A Man Named
FATHER JOZO

Father Jozo has presented many pilgrims with pictures of the statue of Mary in his church. The following is a prayer by Father Jozo blessing these pictures.

O Jesus, Son of God our Father, and of our Mother, please take these pictures in Your hands and bless them. Extend Your blessing so that wherever these pictures are placed no evil can exist. Let peace enter every person who takes this picture of our Mother and holds it. O Jesus, with Your divine hands, bless Your children. Free them from bondage and evil. Free them from all fear. Let peace flow out of Your heart and pour into their hearts. O Jesus, heal us with Your peace. Bless Your prophets here and give them the strength and faith of both Moses and David to enable them to trust in You with all their hearts, in all ways to acknowledge You, and You will direct their paths free of fear.

Gospa, bless all your children. . .your dear ones. We all need you. Fill our hearts with your love. Be a Mother to all these pilgrims and to their families and countries. Dear Mother, we do not want to leave this place without taking you with us. Please come with us and be a Mother to us, our families, our church and our country; and be a Mother of our hopes and prayers; a Mother of our love. O Gospa, bless us. O Jesus, the Son of God our Father and of our Mother, please let Your blessing flow out of Your hands for us. At the request of Your holy Mother, please give us peace.

In the Name of the Father, and of the Son, and of the Holy Spirit. Amen.
Holy Mother and Queen of Peace, pray for us.

Follow this Prayer with The Apostles Creed and 7 Our Father's, 7 Hail Mary's and 7 Glory Be's.

A Man Named
FATHER JOZO

His Story, His Talks, and
The Production of the Film
"A Call to Holiness"

Compiled, Edited and Published
by
THE RIEHLE FOUNDATION
P.O. BOX 7
MILFORD, OHIO 45150

Published by The Riehle Foundation

Copyright © 1989 The Riehle Foundation

Library of Congress Catalog Card No.: 89-062822

ISBN: 1-877678-06-6

The Riehle Foundation
P.O. Box 7,
Milford, OH 45150

TABLE OF CONTENTS

Statue of Our Lady.

Chapter I
FR. ZOVKO–A CALL TO HOLINESS

In May of 1989, a new video was released by Marian Video Productions entitled "A Call to Holiness." It is a talk by Father Jozo Zovko, and the title totally defines the man.

The story of how that film was produced is detailed in this book. It defines the mystique now emerging from this quiet, soft spoken, special son of Mary.

Who is Fr. Jozo Zovko? Does anyone really know his total role in the apparitions at Medjugorje? Is his major contribution still to come? We believe the latter.

Fr. Jozo was the pastor at St. James Church in Medjugorje, when the apparitions began. He eventually was sent away twice, first by the government through a three year jail sentence, then after his release, by the bishop through assignment to another parish. Yet, his association with the events in Medjugorje continues, and in fact appears to be increasing.

Usually, in our lives, we are not able to discern God's plans, the events taking place at the present, the seemingly foggy outline of an uncertain future. It is only in looking back that we are able to see how events came together, as well as the logic that is usually involved. Is this the case with Fr. Jozo, who seemed to suffer most from the Medjugorje events? Now, after eight years of apparitions, eight years of experiences, one can look back and ask: "Was Fr. Jozo the sacrificial lamb, the holy victim?"

Fr. Jozo came to St. James as pastor only months before the apparitions began. He knew none of the seers, and only a few of the parishioners; and, he initially didn't believe the

1

apparitions were real. In order, he had to contest the seers, the parishioners, the authorities, and his bishop. It is ironic that Fr. Jozo Zovko, who would be sentenced to jail for his belief in the apparitions, would initially oppose the acceptance of the apparitions by Bishop Pavao Zanic (he who would later become the chief adversary). It was Fr. Jozo's ordeal that gave true credence and recognition to the events, and established the pattern of spirituality that would become known worldwide.

Fr. Jozo's experiences through those first few months are almost beyond most of our imaginations. He not only grappled with the event of the apparitions, the crowds they produced, the stability of his parish and the views of his bishop, but he also faced a hostile government set on eliminating this troublesome wave of newly claimed fervor over Christianity, and particularly regarding Croatian Catholics.

Fr. Jozo's experiences through those first two months are adequately covered in several books on the apparitions, notably:

"The Queen of Peace Visits Medjugorje," by Fr. Joseph A. Pelletier (Assumption Publications),

"Spark From Heaven" by Mary Craig (Ave Maria Press),

"Is the Virgin Mary Appearing at Medjugorje?" by Fr. René Laurentin (Word Among Us Press), and,

"Queen of Peace in Medjugorje," by Jacov Marin (The Riehle Foundation).

We recap those early events, using some of these sources.

Chapter II
I DIDN'T BELIEVE

Fr. Jozo Zovko, a forty-year-old handsome and idealistic Franciscan, came to Medjugorje on November 11, 1980. The change was very difficult for him and he missed his previous parish in Posusje, in north-western Hercegovina. Initially, he was disappointed in the parishioners' lukewarm response to the changes he was trying to implement. He was convinced of the value of prayer groups and the need to bring the Holy Spirit into the individual lives of the parishioners. He stressed an increased prayer life. Instead, he had found a somewhat less than fervent superfluous traditionalism, and one that did not see a great need to incorporate change. The parishioners did not see a need to "fast" or increase time of prayer or other things not mandated by the Church, yet they were comfortable with being Catholic, a tradition that spans centuries.

Fr. Jozo knew only a few of the parishioners, and found difficulty in attracting the youth to the Sacraments and to prayer meetings and catechism classes. He knew none of the eventual visionaries, except by sight. The unfolding of the heavenly plan had begun.

Prior to his transfer to Medjugorje, Fr. Jozo had arranged to preach several week long retreats at other areas. From June 17 to June 24th, 1981, he was leading a retreat for the sisters in Klostar Ivanic, in northern Croatia. From there he was to go to a renewal group meeting in Zagreb; then a stop at his former parish in Posusje. It was there that he learned that a lightning storm in Medjugorje had caused a fire which burned down the utilties building, which explained his unsuccessful attempts to reach St. James Parish by phone. And so he had been removed from all contact with Medjugorje on June 24th

3

and 25th when the apparitions began, an event that would shake the world.

Upon returning to Medjugorje, he must have had a great shock. Cars and people were everywhere, and what he had heard, enroute, in Mostar was confirmed: "Six children are saying that Our Lady is appearing to them."

Fr. Jozo's ordeal had begun.

According to the above referenced books, Fr. Jozo is portrayed as being distrustful of irrational supernatural occurences. He is analytical and rooted in the essentials—the Mass, the Sacraments. During his first week back at Medjugorje, amid alternating chaos and exuberance, Fr. Jozo attempted to give some stability to the events. With information and assistance from his assistant Fr. Zrinko, he questioned the seers at length, trying to establish some validity to the claims of some that it was all just a trick, or that the children were on drugs. He avoided going to the hill of the apparitions, discouraged others from going and attempted to bring the crowds of people into the church instead, believing that discernment could only be found there, in the Sacraments. His attempts were largely ignored at the outset, and would be made more difficult by the eventual public support of the apparitions by Bishop Zanic.

Fr. Jozo states that, in the beginning, he did not believe. He faced only this great horde of people, now numbering in the thousands, and all bypassing the church to climb the hill. Many returned disillusioned because they saw no vision, no miracle. Was it all someone's trick? Worse yet, was it the work of Satan? The government suspected some religious conspiracy, concocted by this new parish priest, and being used to stir up the people to return to the old ways, days of insurrection, terror, and conflict with the government.

On Monday, June 29th, heavenly intervention again came into play. Fr. Jozo was ordered to appear at a League of Communists headquarters meeting in Citluk. The authorities had not been able to suppress these gatherings on the hill and the scornful reports, now being produced by the media, were only bringing more people to the site. Amid hostility and threats, the authorities finally requested that the crowds be controlled by moving them into the church. The evening Mass, which was to become a legend in its own time, had just been sanctioned for St. James Parish, by the opponents.

But what of these alleged apparitions? Is she appearing, or isn't she? The burden of Fr. Jozo had not been lessened in that regard. He still feared some eventual collapse of the whole event. And what then of his parish, and of the Church? Fr. Jozo's moment of truth came on July 1st and 2nd.

On Wednesday, July 1, in the afternoon, Fr. Jozo was alone in the church, kneeling in the pew and praying. Actually, he was there every afternoon, alone, and praying while the people rushed by the church to the hill, urged by curiosity. All this curiosity and wishing for sensationalism, bothered and offended his soul very much, especially when he heard people swearing when they returned from the hill after not seeing anything. He did not feel the necessity to go there himself. He was alone in the church. He prayed and meditated, prayed the psalms from the breviary, sifting his soul for some events in the history of our redemption. He remembered the troubles of Abraham, Moses. . .

"My God, this multitude of people gathers here, amasses here in my parish. I feel it as a big ordeal. What do I have to do?" He was afraid that perhaps Satan was using this, that the enemies of the religion were using it. "God, if you wish something from these people, if you wish something from me, I am ready, tell me!"

And he prayed in this way, truly praying with his whole heart, aware of his responsibility before God, before his conscience, before the whole Church. He felt that he must be there and pray and wait for a sign from God to show him what to do—he suddenly heard a voice very clearly, as if someone were standing right next to him saying:

"Go out now and protect the children!"

He immediately stood up from the pew and headed out of the church through the center door. As he took hold of the doorknob and was opening the door, and just as he took one step out, all of a sudden the children-seers, all six of them, pasted themselves to him like a swarm of bees: "The police are after us, hide us!"

He hurried the children to the rectory, unlocked the doors and hid the children in an empty room which no one used. "Stay here, calm down and keep quiet!" He had just come out of the house and saw three militia men running by the church. They stopped and asked him: "Did you see the children?" "I did!" Then they kept on running toward Bijakovici, and the children remained in the house.

That afternoon, the children saw their apparition in the clergy house: "We began to pray," said Vicka, "and in a moment the Virgin appeared to us. She prayed a bit with us and sang a bit. She said we'd come through all right and not to be afraid."

The next day, before Holy Mass, the seers were leading the rosary, kneeling behind the altar. And during the praying of the rosary, Our Lady appeared in the church. She hovered above the people, at the back above the entrance, in front of the choir loft. She appeared above all the people. It seems that the pastor, Fr. Zovko, too, saw Our Lady.

He became a new man. From that day forward Fr. Jozo led St. James parish in total conversion. It was a fire that drew its nourishment from biblical images. It was the first wave of many conversions, all based on prayer, fasting, forgiveness and peace. Fr. Jozo was to begin a renewal movement to be felt around the world.

During the Mass he gave a sermon about conversion, about the ways that lead to God, and especially about fasting, penance and prayer. An enormous mass of people listened and absorbed the Word of God. It seemed as if they were hearing it for the first time. It fell like drops of rain on a dry and thirsty ground and created in them a new spirit and a new heart.

According to Fr. Jozo, that Mass was the greatest miracle in Medjugorje that he ever saw. He later stated, "It was THE moment of conversion for the entire parish." In a single day the parish had suddenly and completely returned to God.

From then on, his conviction as to the apparitions, and the

homilies he preached, had started an unprecedented wave of confessions and participation in the Mass. Evening services were suddenly lasting three to four hours. Sometimes, a portion of the people remained all night in the church. Fr. Jozo had suddenly brought living meaning to the word renewal. It also brought about his arrest.

Along with increased religious fervor, this new phase of the Medjugorje apparitions brought extreme hostility and tensions. The authorities, now certain Fr. Jozo was creating a political uprising, banned access to the hill. On August 11th, 1981, Fr. Jozo was again called to party headquarters and ordered to stop the people from continuing to go up the hill and to abolish the evening Mass. He could not comply.

In early August 1981, he told his assistant: "Be prepared to take over my job." Fr. Jozo foresaw his fate.

On August 17th, the expected visit came and Fr. Jozo was arrested and charged with conspiracy. He later stated,

> "My going to prison was no accident but it had nothing to do with my being stubborn or provoking the authorities. It was the logical result of the choices we all have to make at some stage of our lives."

> "Every good priest," he said, "should see the inside of a jail and suffer for the faith. I discovered in prison what the Catholic faith is, and the strength and dignity of a life being offered."

During the first weeks of the apparitions, the seer, Ivanka, had said to Fr. Jozo: "The only ones who do not believe us are the priests and the police." The events had come full cycle.

On October 22nd Fr. Jozo was sentenced to three years in prison. At the same time, two other Franciscans, Fathers Ferdo Vlasic and Jozo Krizic, (publishers of a Franciscan publication) were also given multiple year sentences for contributing to the alleged uprising.

In his book, "Messages and Teachings of Mary at Medjugorje," Fr. René Laurentin cites several conversations of the seers with the Madonna regarding Fr. Jozo during that period

of his trial and imprisonment. The messages of Our Lady
were as follows:

SATURDAY, AUGUST 8TH, 1981

*Do penance! Strengthen your faith through prayer and the
sacraments.* (D.).

MONDAY, AUGUST 17TH

*Do not be afraid. I wish that you would be filled with joy
and that the joy could be seen on your faces. I will protect
Father Jozo.* (The latter was the pastor of the parish at Medjugorje who was imprisoned). (BL.338).

SATURDAY, AUGUST 22ND

Father Jozo has nothing to fear. All that will pass. (DV.1, 3).

FRIDAY, AUGUST 28TH

At the hour of the apparitions, the seers wait in the room
of Fr. Jozo, who is in prison. The Virgin does not appear.
It is the second time that this has happened. They go to church
and pray. She appears to them:

*I was with Father Jozo. That is why I did not come. Do
not trouble yourselves if I do not come. It suffices then to
pray.* (DV.1, 5).

SATURDAY, AUGUST 29TH

Jakov: "How is Ivan in prison?"[1]
*He is well. He is enduring everything. All that will pass.
Father Jozo sends you greetings.* (DV.1).
"What is the news from our village?"
My angels, you are doing your penance well.
"Will you help us in our studies?"
God's help manifests itself everywhere.
*Go in the peace of God with the blessing of Jesus and mine.
Goodbye.* (Ivan's Journal: C76).

---

1. Ivan Ivankovic, son of Pero, and cousin of Vicka, one of the four men at
   Bijakovici who bear this name. He had been arrested by the police August
   12th, on the hill of the apparitions, and imprisoned.

Ivanka: "Will you leave us a sign soon?"
Again, a little patience. (DV.1).

MONDAY, OCTOBER 12TH

I will not yet leave the sign. I shall continue to appear. Father Jozo sends you greetings. He is experiencing difficulties, but he will resist, because he knows why he is suffering. (CP, 18: DV.2, 10).

MONDAY, OCTOBER 19TH

Pray for Father Jozo and fast tomorrow on bread and water. Then you will fast for a whole week on bread and water. Pray, my angels. Now I will show you Father Jozo. (CP 20).

The seers have a vision of Fr. Jozo in prison. He tells them not to be afraid for him, that everything was well.

With respect to Marinko who protected the visionaries:

There are a few similar faithful. He has made a sufficient number of sacrifices for Father Jozo. He underwent many torments and sufferings. Continue, and do not let anyone take the faith away from you.

WEDNESDAY, OCTOBER 21ST

With respect to Fr. Jozo who, while in jail, is awaiting sentence from the court:

Vicka: "Dear Gospa, I know that you do not have the spirit of vengeance, but try nevertheless to bring certain people to reason, so that they might judge impartially."

Jozo looks well and he greets you warmly. Do not fear for Jozo. He is a saint, I have already told you. (CP. 21).

"Will Jozo be condemned?"

Sentence will not be pronounced this evening. Do not be afraid, he will not be condemned to a severe punishment. Pray only, because Jozo asks from you prayer and perseverance. Do not be afraid because I am with you. (DV. 2, 14).

THURSDAY, OCTOBER 22ND

Jozo has been sentenced. Let us go to church to pray.
"We were sad because of Jozo."
You should rejoice! (DV. 2, 14; CP. 21).

"Is the whiteness of the cross a supernatural phenomenon?"
Yes, I confirm it. (DV. 2, 15; CP. 21).

After many people saw the cross on Mt. Krizevac transform
itself into a light, then into a silhouette of the Virgin:
*All of these signs are designed to strengthen your faith until
I leave you the visible and permanent sign.* (F2, 155).

For what was Fr. Jozo supposedly to suffer? How often did
Our Lady visit with him? And what did he know of the future
events of Medjugorje?

Fr. Jozo admits to having a vision of Our Lady in early
July, the time of his profound and dramatic turn-around in
the acceptance of the apparitions. He seldom speaks about
it, or about those many long months in prison. Those who
know him well believe he experienced additional meetings with
Our Lady in some fashion during that time. He only states:

"Prison locks are no proof against God's power.
No one can take faith away, nor deny the action
of grace. You cannot truly imprison anyone who
believes. At the very moment when one has lost
everything, he finds his greatest strength."

Strong pressure was brought to bear on the government, and
hundreds of letters, many from outside of Yugoslavia, obtained
a reduction in Fr. Jozo's sentence. He was released from prison
in the spring of 1983, after 18 months imprisonment.

He did not remain long at St. James Parish in Medjugorje
after his return. The apparitions, by this time, had attracted
worldwide attention. Millions were making their way to that
remote little village. Moreover, Bishop Zanic changed his original favorable opinion of the events and had emerged as the
prime adversary and antagonist.

Fr. Jozo was transferred and became the pastor of St. Elijah
Church, in Tihaljina, Yugoslavia, some 15 to 20 miles from
Medjugorje.

Prayer In The Homes

Every Day The Rosary Is Prayed

Prayer By The Young

And In The Fields

Fr. Jozo

Prayer Before Our Lady

Prayer For The Pilgrims

Our Lady

The Village

The Valley At The Base Of Mt. Krizevac

Fr. Jozo In The Church At Tihaljina

Fr. Jozo Meets With Pilgrims

Statue Of Our Lady

St. Elijah Church In Tihaljina

Chapter III
SUFFERING SERVANT

From his earliest struggles with his former parish at Medjugorje, through the early chaotic weeks of the apparitions, and finally through 18 months of imprisonment, Fr. Jozo embodies the image of Jesus' suffering servant.

The eight years, since June 24, 1981, give us great hindsight to the role he played, the sacrifices he endured, the beginnings he nurtured. Yet, Fr. Jozo still is the quiet voice, the blooming rose not yet opened. He is seldom in the spotlight, nor has he written a book. The other priests who have been assigned to St. James during the period of the apparitions have addressed millions of pilgrims, providing hundreds of profound talks and material, both taped and printed. Yet the deep reflections of Fr. Jozo, for the most part, do not often surface.

Still, there are those who believe Fr. Jozo knows something more about Medjugorje, maybe even its future. How often has Mary appeared to him? And with what messages? He speaks about Medjugorje with a certainty that is both consoling yet inspiring.

Few, outside of the seers, realized a more dramatic conversion than did Fr. Jozo through his discernment of the apparitions. Yet, though hundreds of interviews with the seers have been made public, he has remained in the background. It is true that Fr. Jozo's prison release included restrictions on his being re-assigned to Medjugorje in the future, and promoting the apparitions as in his former position. But the past few years have somewhat altered that course. Now Medjugorje is seemingly coming to him.

It is now very common for pilgrims to visit Fr. Jozo during

their stay in Medjugorje. They come from all over the world. They find a man of deep reflection, of intense spirituality. His commitment, his faith, his belief show through. He is quiet, soft spoken, bringing out prayer and spiritual food from deep within his being.

He reflects a deep love and adoration for his Saviour, and a dedication to the Mother of Christ that is unshakable, that seems to be beyond mere human values or proofs. He speaks with a certain conviction, like he has come to understand all which we have to accept on pure faith alone. He is a man of intense devotion, intense peace—saintly.

Those who visit him seem to sense these qualities. They seem to sense a supernatural presence that transcends words, or even language. He does not speak English, yet English speaking pilgrims are often-times spellbound.

In his parish, St. Elijah, Fr. Jozo has a beautiful statue of Mary. It is the "Immaculate Conception." Generally, it is described as the most beautiful statue of Mary anyone has ever seen, and is becoming as popular as Fr. Jozo himself to the camera lenses of countless visitors. (see footnote)

Recently, there are claims that this special image of Our Lady may have taken on additional significance, with reported cures and spiritual healings attributed to Our Lady's and Fr. Jozo's intercession.

Eight years have taken some toll on Medjugorje. It was to be expected. Commercialization of the area (even some of the villagers) eventually surfaced along with the millions and millions of pilgrims. The quiet, serene village is becoming permeated with noise, bus fumes, souvenir shops and restaurants. Fr. Jozo is obviously aware, and saddened by these emerging changes. He often speaks of the rush of an over-zealous mankind to meet his God, and rushing right past the true messages being given at Medjugorje in the process.

Has some divine intervention taken this "suffering servant" away from all that, to the still peaceful and quiet surroundings

---

The statue is also known as "Our Lady of Grace" and "Our Mother of Mercy." Additional background is provided on page 71.

of his current parish? There, a certain amount of solitude, or time for meditation and prayer, is more available. It has become an annex to Medjugorje for Fr. Jozo and the beautiful statue of Our Lady. It has also become a "retreat within a retreat" for the pilgrims who come to Medjugorje. Their visit with Fr. Jozo and his special image of Our Lady is a brief interlude away from the ever increasing activity surrounding St. James Parish.

The story of the production of the film "A Call to Holiness" (referenced at the beginning of this book), is reflective of the charisms of this man, his role in God's plan of salvation, and the continued heavenly intervention. The testimonies of Michael Hall (Medjugorje Witness), and Marian Video Production (producers of the film) are included in this book, as well as the filmed interview. Additionally, included are edited texts of several other of Fr. Jozo's talks given to visiting pilgrimages.

They reflect the deep spiritual commitment of a man named Fr. Jozo.

Chapter IV
WITNESS—MICHAEL HALL

On March 16, 1989, I returned from leading a group of 24 pilgrims to Medjugorje, mostly from my home parish, St. Charles Borromeo, Bloomington, Indiana. Our parish will be forever enriched. Those in our travel group were truly moved by the wonderful pilgrimage experience.

For me, this second visit was a great boost to my faith. I was not so much overwhelmed by the newness of the people or place, or by the many external signs prevalent to pilgrims. This was a journey of the heart. I felt, and now feel, God's presence, through Our Lady, in a profound and truly personal sense. I feel her love and protection in a way that dispells all fear.

Healing was one of the major themes of our pilgrimage. I had the special grace of being given a card containing a piece from a blood-stained glove of Padre Pio, who bore the wounds of the Stigmata for 50 years of his priesthood in Italy. The woman who gave me this relic described how Padre Pio had wrapped strips from this glove around the wrists of her crippled hands, which now are healed.

As pilgrims we visited Fr. Jozo during our pilgrimage stay in Medjugorje. Fr. Jozo ended his talk by blessing, then distributing, picture cards of the statue of Mary, "Mother of Mercy." This statue resides at St. Elijah Church, his current parish, in Tihaljina, about 20 miles from Medjugorje. He told of receiving a letter from a woman who had prayed with the card over a three-year-old with AIDS. She wrote that the AIDS has been removed. Another letter told of a person with terminal cancer who had been cured in a similar fashion. Fr. Jozo then encouraged all present to become instruments of God's healing.

Finally, I visited the family of a child from Medjugorje. In October, 1987, Fr. Bernie Weber of Fairfield, Alabama, had led a prayer asking for healing for the child's inability to keep her balance. A number from our present pilgrimage had participated in that prayer. This same family was now showing us this same child, completely normal, a healing they said that began right after that prayer two years ago.

When I heard Fr. Jozo speak, I was deeply moved by his holiness and his message. For me, Fr. Jozo is the most compelling figure among all the special people at Medjugorje. How I wished we could have a videotape of his talk. I was led to call the organizers of the National Conference on Medjugorje to ask if such a film might be helpful to them. They were excited, and encouraged me to pursue the project.

I began to make arrangements to send over a film crew. But first I was advised to consult a number of Medjugorje leaders, to see if such a tape already existed, or if a TV crew might be scheduled to go to Medjugorje soon. One of the centers I called was the Riehle Foundation. They agreed to explore further and encouraged me in my task.

Several days later, from out of the blue, I received a call from Anne McGlone of Marian Video in Philadelphia. Both Anne and her company were totally unknown to me. Anne said, "I understand you are interested in a video of Fr. Jozo. We have the footage you're looking for. Tell us what to do!"

I was absolutely stunned by her words, and remained speechless for about 30 seconds. Finally, I said, "Excuse me, this comes as quite a shock. Tell me more."

She said Fr. Jozo had granted them a private interview at St. Elijah's in November 1987. He had spoken (without an interpretor) for 45 minutes in Croatian. They had been waiting for an inspiration on how to use this footage, which had never been fully translated.

I had Anne send me a copy of the film. Since Indiana University, located in my hometown, has one of the best Slavic language departments in the country, it was possible to quickly complete the translation. From there, the film went into production in Philadelphia. What had appeared to require months to formulate, if possible at all, was now being completed in a matter of days.

Now that "A Call To Holiness" is completed, I can attest to the power and eloquence of its message. As Fr. Jozo encouraged us, I encourage you: Use this film as a source of God's healing! My eternal thanks to Our Lady, Queen of Peace, and to her Son, Our Lord Jesus, for the honor of being part of this effort.

Michael Hall
Medjugorje Witness
Bloomington, IN

Chapter V
WITNESS OF MARIAN VIDEO PRODUCTIONS

Murray Bodo, O.F.M. once wrote, "as we journey through life, we not only leave something behind, but we gain something as well. For as we embark upon a journey to God, we are aware of how far we really are from Him for Whom we long, toward Whom we are journeying."

No words could better express the journey of Marian Video Productions in producing the latest video entitled *A Call to Holiness,* an intimate prayer experience and interview with Fr. Jozo Zovko, O.F.M.

It is a video extraordinaire called forth by Our Lady through incredibly mystifying circumstances.

In November 1987, the Marian Video production crew traveled to Tihjalina, Yugoslavia to interview Fr. Jozo Zovko in his current parish. Arriving at his parish in total faith, we had not planned any specific interview nor had we prepared a set of questions for the interview. Father did not even know we were arriving for an interview. We decided, in prayer, to proceed on faith and take the cameras to his parish not knowing even if we would encounter him. We simply trusted. Upon arriving, our interpreter knocked on the rectory door and introduced all of us. He asked our intentions in interviewing him. We told him, through our interpreter, we wanted just to hear his story, the story of Medjugorje. He agreed to meet us in a building to the left of the church. As we awaited his arrival, we went inside his church to pray. There we discovered the beautiful statue of Our Mother of Mercy. It is breathtaking. Immediately the crew shot footage of the statue and the inside of the church. As we finished with the statue and the cross, Fr. Jozo summoned us to a small building. He asked

17

us to close the doors behind us and politely asked us not to leave the room. He, obviously, was apprehensive about the interview. We knew, at that moment, he was fearful. Of what, we were uncertain. It would be foolish for us to speculate on why the door had to be locked and why we were not permitted to leave until he was finished.

What happened behind those doors is history. Fr. Jozo, without the aid of an interpreter began sharing his personal, intimate story of the happenings in Medjugorje. There were seven of us present in the room. All of us felt the power of the Spirit through Fr. Jozo. Even though we didn't know what he was saying, since he was speaking in Croatian, we knew within our hearts he was sharing a powerful message. Amidst the tears of Fr. Jozo, our camera's were turned off to allow this man of God to weep in community with us. It was a moment of healing.

He finished sharing his story and then prayed for those who will watch this video. We were all moved to tears. He left the room and offered snacks for us in the rectory. We could barely leave the room, the annointing was heavy. As we walked over to the rectory, our interpreter told us Mary guided him in his prayer and, that she was present in the room. We were speechless and overwhelmed.

As we shared in special snacks prepared by a woman in the rectory, Fr. Jozo walked into the room and offered to pray with each of us. As we departed from his holy presence, I remember turning around to kiss him on the cheek. Tears were running down his face as he bid us farewell.

We had just experienced a "reed of God," a transmitter of His love. As we drove away, the annointing stayed with us.

After returning to the United States in November, 1987 we embarked on producing two Medjugorje video tapes. The first tape entitled *"Reaching Heavenly Dimensions"* was produced for a local Catholic radio audience. Our second video entitled *"Transforming Your Heart"* is now distributed internationally. Our third video entitled *"Kibeho, Africa—Mary Speaks to the World"* is also being distributed internationally. And now, Mary has called forth *"A Call to Holiness."*

In producing two videotapes on Medjugorje, we were never led to use the Fr. Jozo footage. We used a student at the University of Pennsylvania, a native of Yugoslavia, to translate Fr. Jozo's interview. All of this was recorded on a microcassette. Yet, we were never inspired to use the footage. That is, until a simple phone call was placed to Frances Reck of the Riehle Foundation concerning business. It was, within this call, that she mentioned a gentleman by the name of Michael Hall, Bloomington, Indiana, who happened to be searching for a crew to send back to Medjugorje to produce a video on Fr. Jozo. Michael Hall experienced great healing and power through Fr. Jozo and he wanted to bring Fr. Jozo to the United States through video.

As Fran shared how Michael wanted to tape Fr. Jozo, I said to her, "Fran, we have Fr. Jozo on tape. . .close to one hour. It has been sitting on our shelves since 1987. We have been praying and waiting for the right moment to make a tape using this footage." We both laughed knowing Mary was at work again connecting her people. Fran gave me Mike's number.

When Michael Hall answered the telephone in his office and heard my unknown voice telling him we had footage of Fr. Jozo, he was stunned. So were we, at Marian Video. Then, the whole process began. . .the amazing story of calling forth individuals to participate with us in producing this video. Michael Hall heard the call from Mary. He took the "first step in faith." He entrusted us with the vision of bringing Fr. Jozo to the United States on video. We had met another man of God willing to serve selflessly, just wanting to serve Our Lady, Queen of Peace.

Michael took our VHS dub and had it translated in Indiana. Within one week, editing was underway. As Drew and I assembled this video we were worried in keeping the viewer interested in a sit-down interview. After all, Fr. Jozo did not allow us to shoot him walking or talking outside of the interview. We had, simply, a sit-down interview. How in the world could we ever make this interesting?

So, we prayed, "Mary, our Mother, guide us in this video. Show us what you want us to do." She answered our prayers immediately. She sent us Tony Cilento of Milwaukee, Wisconsin. Again, we had never heard of him. Tony is a professional photographer owning his own studio. Michael Hall told us about how Tony had just taken more than 6,000 slides in Medjugorje. Thank You Lord. Tony, acting in faith sent a set of slides to us, express mail. Needless to say, his slides provide a perfect backdrop for Fr. Jozo's sharing and prayer.

Then, music became a prime consideration. Music, music. . .where could we find a professional track recording with no money. Enter Grace Markay, professional recording artist who had recorded under Capital Records in the secular music industry.

Today, she records Christian music under GOOD SHEPHERD RECORDS in Philadelphia. Grace had recorded a song entitled *I Had Nothing Left to Give*, on her new album I CLING TO YOU. Well, as soon as we heard it we knew it was our theme song. And, Grace was thrilled to have us use her music. Not only this, her arranger and composer of the song, Richie Rome, had just finished an album with Dionne Warwick. He is an award-winning arranger. All this in five days.

Then, we had to overcome the major, major problem. Who would be the voice of Fr. Jozo on the tape? We needed a voice to hold the audience. . .someone who would act just like Fr. Jozo. . .a voice with a healing tonal quality. Enter Paul Springle, a professional man who uses his voice on some of the famous television commercials. Trust, total trust. Paul Springle was the ideal choice as narrator. He became Fr. Jozo to us, capturing our hearts with his narration. Thanks again Lord.

Now, one must remember that we, at Marian Video, are literally a small operation. So, when we produce a tape, we also have to answer the mail, lick the stamps, answer the telephone, and design jackets for the tapes too. It is just two of us. . .and, two volunteers who help us during the week. In the middle of a weekend editing session, it finally dawned on the two of us that we had forgotten about having the jackets of the tape designed. And, what in the world would the name of the tape be? After much prayer the name evolved, *A Call to Holiness*. And, the jacket for the tape was designed in post haste and sent to New York for printing. Now, the largest obstacle hit us. The printer couldn't possibly have the jackets ready in a few days to be sent to the duplicator. We trusted again. It's another "okay, Mary" moment. As we finished the tape in the post-production house, the very moment the tape was finished the printer in New York called and said all of his machinery broke down. "Here we go, satan. Get behind us. This is Mary's work and you have no authority on this one."

As it turned out, the printer beat his own deadline, the tape was finished on time. Mary helped us beat all the odds. . .again . . .and, again!

Yet, the most powerful part of this story is the dream sequence Mary gave Drew and myself in preparation for editing. Three nights before we began editing, Drew experienced a dream in which Mary materialized out of a statue into a real, live person talking to him. And, I experienced Mary speaking to me saying, "remember the message of Fatima in all the work you do." As we processed these two events, it became quite clear that Mary wanted us to add an "Act of Consecration" to this video. She showed us the way and, we know this was totally inspired by her. It would never have occurred to us to incorporate a consecration prayer in a Fr. Jozo video.

All-in-all, Mary guided our hearts in producing this video. She called forth a team of individuals to be involved, utilizing gifts of photography, voice, music, camera, editing and prayer. We have no idea what she plans with this video. We were simply her instruments in bringing it into life. . .now, as we sit and wait for our next project, we pray for all those touched by this tape to be healed and transformed. We pray you are called to a new path of holiness through Jesus and Mary.

Anne McGlone
Marian Video
Lima, PA

Chapter VI
A CALL TO HOLINESS

The following is the text of the November 1987 interview of Jr. Jozo which became the video, "A Call to Holiness." Produced by Marian Video Productions of Lima, PA, in conjunction with Medjugorje Witness, Inc. of Bloomington, IN, it was released in May 1989. Fr. Jozo begins with a prayer.

In the name of the Father, and the Son, and the Holy Spirit, Amen. Oh Lord, we feel your presence among us. This Catholic television program wants to make its contribution to your Church. Give this Church a new seed of love, grace and truth, the love by which you love us, and the truth by which you make us free.

Oh Father, send us your Holy Spirit. Send your Spirit to us who have gathered here. Send the Holy Spirit to all those who will watch this program in order to receive your message. Through these words, which are weak and incomplete, let them hear your words, which are spontaneous, which are love and peace, which are miraculous.

Oh God, send us the Holy Spirit so that we all can accept the truth and the power of your heavenly word. Oh, send us your Holy Spirit. You promised this through the prophet who said, "I will give you my Spirit who will remove your heart of stone and give you a new heart, a heart of flesh."

Father, first you gave such a heart to your son Jesus, our brother. . .

† *A heart full of love for everybody, especially sinners,*

† *A heart that forgave everybody, especially the evil ones,*

† *A heart that was able to embrace the cross,*

22

✝ *A heart that knew how to be humble and obedient unto death.*

Oh Lord, give us such a heart, a heart of flesh, full of compassion and love. Oh God, let this filming be in your hand at this very moment, so that it will light the fire in our heart and, by the power of your Spirit, do what you have promised; to transform us, to change our hearts.

Jesus, you had a wonderful, pure heart, but ours is impure. Purify our heart. You had a humble heart, but ours is arrogant and proud. Oh, renew our heart. Make it free to love.

Our Lady, pray for us, pray with us. Those gathered here in your name, and for you, ask you to pray with us. We ask the Holy Spirit to dwell within us, as with the apostles in the room of the last supper. Let the Holy Spirit fill us, too.

Our Lady, you prayed with the apostles. You have remained the eternal mother of our Church. You pray in our Church and for our Church. Oh, pray with us now, so that through your prayer of love your grace will enter our hearts, and the hearts of those who will watch this.

Oh Lady, our consolation in sorrow, let the people who will watch this program be consoled. Ignite the beliefs and hopes of all the people who have lost them. Illuminate their hearts. Fill them with trust. All who are searching for love, who feel that they have lost their love, let them find it again for you. Oh Lady, for all who seek their peace, who have lost peace in their families, let them find peace in you, the Queen of Peace. This peace is your promise to all of us, all who are your children.

Oh, God, Our Lady prays with us, and for us, so that your peace would flow through us, so your Holy Spirit can illuminate our hearts and make us new. Oh Lord, send us your Spirit to fill us entirely, to regenerate us completely, to make us new. Oh Lady, with you and in the name of your son, we will all pray together for this wonderful gift of Heaven, this gift that was promised to the Church, this gift of the Holy Spirit.

✝   ✝   ✝

Six years, four months, and eighteen days ago, Our Lady surprised us by choosing our small village to be a new Bethlehem. She surprised not only the villagers, but also me as the parish priest of Medjugorje, and the whole world. Like other interventions of Heaven, it did not happen with a boom, like a landslide that slides downhill. No, a powerful seed was planted, a surprise of love which began to grow in our hearts. A surprise of grace which began to release faith and love in our hearts. This seed began to grow. Our Mother knew how to help it grow.

I had not been at home for a day and a half. I was finishing a spiritual retreat for Franciscans in Zagreb. I was shocked by the news of what was happening and I could not believe. I did not believe what the children were saying. I was scared to return to Medjugorje under such strange circumstances. I was afraid the children were not telling the truth. I was afraid of lies. Perhaps the children were talked into this by nonbelievers, by those who could manipulate them. I was scared that the children might be sick. When I spoke with them, I felt they were happy, but I was afraid to share their happiness and joy because I was not sure whether they were telling the truth. My fear was too strong. I tape recorded each word and listened to it day and night when I had time. It brought hundreds of questions to my mind.

Many friends were trying hard to free me of my doubts, both parishioners and priests. The bishop himself made five short visits to Medjugorje before I went to jail. He tried very hard to persuade me that it was true. He preached with a strong voice. He preached his belief that the children were telling the truth—that we have to believe them, that we have to follow what they say. I was sad listening to his words. I felt sorrow listening to his statements, by which he tried to justify his conviction. He was angry that I would not believe him. But I wanted to be honest. How could I say that I believed if I felt that I did not. But they were all certain of their belief. They all hoped I would come to accept that their visions were real, but I could not. Why? All my fears would not let me believe it.

Later I understood. I understood why Jesus asks people, the adult Christians, all his followers, to be like children, to be simple and small. The children in my parish believed it immediately. The young people believed the visionaries. They did not envy them, and they said they were telling the truth. Only I, the parish priest, could not believe them. But Jesus demands us to be small, and obedient. An arrogant man cannot believe; he cannot accept such a simple yet magnificent, sublime and divine truth that we speak with Our Lady. You see, only children who are obedient can believe that. Jesus is right when He wants this.

My experience here is that Our Lady followed the way that was chosen by Jesus. This is the way of being simple, small, humble. My experience in Medjugorje was not a struggle against something or somebody, against unknown powers. This was not a struggle against Communism. Our Lady would not purposely choose a Communist country, a country that hates religion, that banishes religion. No, she did not choose this country because of that.

I do not really know why she chose this country or place. I know roughly the history of this region, which is written in the blood of martyrs, marked by hundreds of years of oppression by Turks, and later by other invaders. I know well the history of our Church, which became famous by hastening to give testimony to the love of Jesus. I know that Our Lady chose this land and this poor place, a tiny village without anything else that could be admired. We could not turn our eyes to anything else except one great treasure, to Our Lady.

So now, people from all over the world gather here. Our Lady chose an interesting approach. In my experience, she has revealed a plan which is being accomplished with prayer, fasting, and meeting Jesus in church through the sacraments.

At the beginning, as I can easily recall, Our Lady said: "Please be converted." I thought I understood Our Lady. I thought Our Lady was calling those who left the Church. She was saying, return to Church. To convert means to go back to Church. I thought Our Lady was calling those who did not pray: "Convert, start praying." I thought she was calling those who did not attend the Holy Mass: "Go to Church and celebrate the Holy Mass." I thought she was calling those who were beating their families, or abusing alcohol. I thought this was what Our Lady wanted: Sinners, try to convert.

But Our Lady brought a surprise in this. She said: "I am calling *you*, my son. Why are you looking to them?" I understood only part of it. She did not want to address those who were lost, but to awaken those who were close. When she saw I did not understand what conversion means, she said: "Pray, pray." Well, we prayed. Then she said she would appear in the church. So people gathered there and she did appear. While we prayed she said: "Pray every day, pray the rosary every day."

People were astonished. They stayed in the church all night. And as we prayed she appeared and gave her blessing to the people gathered. People felt her presence so strongly that the next day her message was spread all over the world by the stream of love and enthusiasm coming from our hearts, as it was with our apostles in the gospels.

All the people knew Our Lady wanted us to pray. My entire parish became a chapel in which all the people prayed. Children waiting outside in the street for the bus were praying. Shepherds were praying. People going to the fields were praying. People invited each other not to have coffee but to pray. Children would meet after school was over and pray. They would spend the breaks between classes praying in the schoolyard. On their way to the church they prayed. All Medjugorje had been transformed into a community which was awake in prayer all the time.

I imagined Our Lady would be happy, and she was. But she appeared again and said: "When you pray, do not only say the words, do not only pray with your lips, pray with your heart."

I was thinking what that could mean. I imagined that this could be done through a deep, simple meditation, through extreme concentration and calmness of our mind, or through some other simple activity. Perhaps I had a certain awareness in mind that could guide us in our prayer. Obviously I was mistaken. I was also thinking about other things, as to what prayer with the heart might mean. All my thinking did not help much and I did not know what she was asking for, and she knew it.

Then she sent a message which said: "Before you start praying again today, look within your heart to find all your enemies. Forgive one another. Forgive everybody. Recommend them to our Father with joy. Pray for them. Then wish them a great blessing, joy, and great love."

At first I thought it was not very difficult. I repeated this message in the church, word by word. I asked them whether it was clear what Our Lady wanted. They said they understood. When I asked them whether we were going to do this, the church remained in silence. You can imagine, thousands of people silent in front of me. It was impossible to say yes to Our Lady. They could not lie. Although they met Our Lady every day the people could not say yes. They remained silent.

This was a shock to me, the deep struggle and emptiness of that difficult silence. Not knowing what would happen, I broke into that desert of silence, saying: "Listen to me; now we are going to pray for that gift. Pray in your heart. Close your eyes, go deep down into your hearts and pray to God to grant us the gift to be able to forgive."

The painful silence started again, the struggle inside ourselves. With fear in my heart I began to suspect: "Oh my God, what can I do for these people? We cannot truly pray, if we cannot forgive. Because we cannot forgive, we cannot truly pray. Our Lady does not let us pray our way because this is no true prayer. We cannot wish everybody well." I prayed fervently.

After twenty minutes of this struggle in the desert, Our Lady sent us her gift to break the barrier of silence that had been gripping us. She destroyed the wall and showed us the light. The biggest miracle among so many signs and wonderful moments, among so many changes in people and in nature I have experienced so far in Medjugorje happened that afternoon. As I held all these people in my heart, the greatest sign came.

After twenty minutes, in the middle of the church, a man's voice broke our chains, with a prayer from deep within his soul, a prayer that was Our Lady's gift: "Jesus, I forgive them. Please forgive me." Then he began to cry in a powerful voice.

We all cried together with him. Everybody felt in their heart: I must pray these same words. I have to forgive and ask forgiveness of the people and Jesus. And so we all did the same. That afternoon we were all searching for somebody else's hand, as many hands as possible, to squeeze them and say: "Forgive me." We cried, we are happy and we felt we had been forgiven.

After that we all prayed the rosary. Our Lady gave us a marvelous experience, a great experience, a great mercy and grace. That evening everybody felt that the entire Universe, all the people, prayed with us in our hearts. We felt that our prayer, our holy gift, came out of our hearts and spread all over the world, entering everybody's heart. It brought peace, love, and great joy. After that we celebrated the Holy Mass. That was a great celebration of love, as we could feel so strongly the presence of Jesus alive within us.

The next day the picture of my parish was different. Some parishioners had not spoken to each other for generations, as is the case with all poor peasants all over the world. They had their enemies because of minor irrelevant things. They did not like each other. They were envious and jealous. In one night all that had disappeared, melted, vanished. They began to work and pray together, eat together, love each other sincerely, feel for each other.

On that same day we saw a vision, a banner in the sky spanning from the mountain of the cross to the church towers, saying: "PEACE," with big burning letters. This peace is the immense gift of Our Lady.

I am sad when people do not understand what peace means. I am disappointed when a priest thinks that this is a treaty Reagan and Gorbachev can sign in Geneva. I am sad when

Church people are not able to realize that the Church itself can bring peace, or when a family does not know that their peace can be created itself in their child's heart. They do not know that this peace can be me, or you to me, and myself to you; that I am not the object of envy and jealousy. We do not understand that for us peace can be our Church, our prayer, our sacrament. And my bishop is peace to me, a gift that cannot be given by man because it is God's gift. Our Lady does not want to give us only a tiny bit of it. She wants to give peace to anybody who comes to Medjugorje, to all nations. Our Lady brought peace into our hearts, to each member of our community on that day.

Later she clearly explained that conversion means to pray with the heart: *"To choose the way to conversion means to start praying with your heart."*

Three days later she said, *"Fast."* It was no coincidence. It was not by chance that she spoke about Satan, saying Satan was present; by fasting and prayer you can get rid of him. This was a shock for me, that Satan can be present if Our Lady is here. This was because people could not fully accept her word and the gift of its meaning. Her word was calling people to accept it immediately. We could not do that if we were not free. Free yourself through fasting. Let love live in you through fasting. Overcome all fears by means of fasting. Return to the prophetic belief about fasting.

On that evening (it was Wednesday), I asked people to fast. I told them what Our Lady requested and asked them if they were ready. They all said yes. We fasted on Wednesday, Thursday, Friday, and Saturday. On Friday afternoon the effects were already there. What had bothered me before was that people were not converting. I did not hear one single confession from a nonbeliever on the first day of the fast. After that, crowds of people were coming and asking, "Hear my confession." I was afraid of such a huge crowd wanting confession in the church. I asked all the priests in layman's clothing for help. There were about fifty present. Many of them changed their clothes or put on a clerical sign to hear confessions of

the people gathered in the church. We had confessions throughout the day and all night. In the meantime, more than one
hundred more priests had arrived. This crowd of priests heard
confessions. For the first time, we fully understood the importance of being priests of this holy Sacrament, of this grace
Jesus had left us. Our sleeves were wet from our tears.

People realized for the first time that they could get rid
of their sins without any struggles inside themselves. They
realized that they cannot be judged only by their clothing.
It was the moment when the prodigal son decided to return
to his father. We felt exactly the same. We felt Our Lord's
embrace. We put on that robe which the father had kept for
his son. We felt a thirst for peace, for the love that exists
in our Father's house. So these were the days of the Lord's
true grace.

Our Lady said: *"To convert means to fast with love, to start
fasting with prayer."*

These were my early experiences in Medjugorje: God's magnificent deeds foretold by the prophets. People who know how
to listen will be guided by God. God will show them conversion, grace, the gift of peace and love, the gift of trust, and
the gift of prayer.

So the first thing Our Lady asks of us is to be obedient,
to be subservient as Jesus was according to St. Luke's gospel
and all the gospels of the New Testament. He was obedient
unto His death by crucifixion. To come as a pilgrim to Medjugorje or to hear Our Lady's message means to be humble,
obedient, small.

Our Lady wants to rouse in us the thirst for faith. Many
times she has wept openly here in Medjugorje. It is horrible
to see Our Lady crying. Our Lady's tear is heavy in the sense
of being powerful. It could melt a heart of stone. It could
purify our impure heart and light the fire of joy, light the
fire of peace. It lets somebody live like a little child again.

Therefore, Our Lady does not divide faith into the converted one and the unconverted one, does not divide people
into sinners and believers. She always says, "My dear chil-

dren." So we can feel the majesty of Our Lady, our mother. She recognizes a child in each of us. She does not distinguish between a believer and nonbeliever, a Catholic and non-Catholic. She does not deny anybody.

Everybody is her dear child, everybody who seeks truth, wants to love and be loved. Everybody has to be redeemed and the ransom has been given to all. No Catholic should say: This man is not redeemed as Catholics because Jesus did not name him, so I cannot name him either. We are mistaken if we do not feel like children of our Blessed Mother with the idea that we are all brothers, that we are all children of God, sons and daughters of God, she opened our eyes. Faith is not what we think it is, but what God sees and thinks it is.

Therefore Our Lady told us crying: "Live the faith of the Church." First of all, imagine that she would call us, the priests. That was a shock. She spoke crying: "People do not live the faith of the Church. Tell them to believe firmly, to protect the religion of my people and among my people. Do not have enemies, do not start wars. Let us love everybody and be aware that we are servants." It is dangerous to be in conflict with Heaven, with the Gospel, with Our Lady. It is important to be small. Therefore, we have to live the faith of the Church.

Sentire cum Ecclesias *(in union with the Church)*

This is the principle of the original Church, the principle of every Church, throughout every generation. Our Lady wants people with loving hearts. She transforms people and their hearts, so that all could be Church with one big heart that loves with all the people and is for all the people.

Another thing she told us crying was: "You have forgotten the Bible." Our Lady said: "You have forgotten the Holy Bible." She went on, crying:" Why do you not live the Holy Mass?" She was crying: "Pray for peace." She went on, crying: "The Holy Bible and the Eucharist are the foundations of the Church, its roots." The Church cannot give them up. Then it would live less intensively as an institution. It could exist only with its outer appearance and could not bear any fruit.

The Church must not be separated from the Bible. Our Lady knew that when she said: "The Church has separated from the Bible." You mothers who are watching this program, you know where salt, flour, or bread are in your kitchen. Where is the Bible? When did you last read it together, as a family, or at a gathering of friends? Everybody who listens to God's word and accepts it is like a brother, a sister, or a mother. Our Lady in Medjugorje wants a sister, a daughter, a mother of Jesus who would be able to surrender and serve Jesus, and thus enable His Incarnation. Those who listen to God's word are not lost in darkness. It is necessary to understand the Bible as a light, as the word that illuminates our heart. It helps you realize what your values are; your love, your marriage, your life, your furniture, your car, or your job.

The Holy Mass is the root of our religion, our power, our grace. Through Holy Mass bread and wine are being transformed into God's body and blood, by means of the power of the Spirit, God's Word, and the prayer of the Church. The Church is being transformed. It becomes exactly what God wants, the bread that Jesus sent us saying: *"Take it and eat it."* The Church which lives the Eucharist becomes food, light, and peace for everyone. Therefore, at the end of the Holy Mass, the priest says: Go now, the Holy Mass is over. Go. You are filled with peace because you have received peace. Be bread, the food of peace. Be love because you are the food of love. Since you have enjoyed love, be the bread of love. Go and share it through your life.

We do not know how to live the Holy Mass. We are used to "listening" to the Holy Mass. Our Lady does not want that. We have learned how to "recite" the prayers, but this is not what Our Lady asks for.

Pray with your heart and live the Holy Mass. Listen to God's Word, which is life-giving. Jesus' heart is present in the Bible, which is God's Word. You have to feel God's power and surrender your heart to be able to feel all that love.

According to my experience, Medjugorje is the place where that happens. And you have asked about my experience. Medjugorje gives that to God's children, to his Church. It renews that feeling and brings the grace to put it in our heart.

I would like to ask you to be open when you hear or read the reports about Medjugorje, so that you will not come in conflict with God. Be humble. When Our Lady says something, she is asking us to do it immediately. So be open and trust. She is our mother. She is the one who does not criticize or attack. She does not refuse anybody. She addresses us: "Dear children."

I would like to pray so that from now on her blessing, her prayer and her presence in Medjugorje would be in the hearts of each family in which this film will be seen (or these words are read).

Oh Lady, here we are, your dear children. We could feel only a small piece of your word and your love. You will add the rest. Thank you. Thank you for spreading your arms above us and touching the hearts of your children, and filling our hearts with your blessing.

Jesus, Our Lady's Son, Son of God, Father's Son and man's Son, bless us here. Bless all in America, all American families. Bless the Catholic Church that was sent to hold the light, to plant the seeds of your faith, your presence. Give that seed the power, the power to grow, which will fill America with Your gospel, Your holiness, Your grace and love. Open, oh Jesus, Your heart. Fill all their hearts with love. For You, oh Good Shepherd, protect all the families and provide them with light so that they would know and feel its greatness. Give them peace, so that they can feel the peace which comes from Your heart. Let them feel the joy which is You, Your presence.

Oh Jesus, Your mother prays with us and for us, for all America and all the world. Bless us, bless those who will spread Your love to others. Let them feel joy in their hearts, peace in their lives, and blessing in their families. According to the plea of the sinless mother, bless us, Oh Mighty God; Father, Son, and Holy Spirit. Amen.

Chapter VII
YOUR PILGRIMAGE, WHAT DOES IT MEAN?

(A homily given May 24, 1988, at St. Elijah Parish, Tihaljina, Yugoslavia.)

There is a difference between a tourist and a pilgrim. A tourist is one who sightsees. A pilgrim is a prophet, one called by God, like Moses, to climb Mt. Sinai, meet God and free His people.

The other day I watched it raining. Some of the rain fell on the road and ran off into the gutter. Other drops fell into the river and went to the sea. Some disappeared in the earth. Some drops fell on roses in a garden and nourished them. Yet all the drops came from the same cloud. What happened depended on the place where they fell. So on your pilgrimage, some will get nothing out of it, some will receive pearls of love and peace and joy. It depends on you. But it is the same Medjugorje for all.

Our Lady has transformed Medjugorje. It speaks one language, the language of Our Lady. Medjugorje has become big. People from all nations have come to it. What the UN tried to do and could not, Our Lady has succeeded in doing in a short time. She has made of all nations, one family.

When the disciples went to Emmaus, Jesus went into their hearts and destroyed their short view of things. He opened up Moses and all the prophets to them, and showed how the Messiah had to suffer to enter into glory. They all knew of Moses and the prophets; how come they did not know this? Why don't we?

What is Medjugorje really? I confess that I was one of the last to believe.

The first apparition occurred about two in the afternoon, Ivanka was the first to see Our Lady. Everybody knew her, for she had lost her mother just a month before. I was sad for her. She was like an orphan. She had been herding sheep, like the other children, when she saw a big light. She thought it was a fire on the hill, Podbrdo. The light was like a big wall. Mirjana was with her. They were afraid of this big light and both of them ran away. Then Ivanka turned back and looked again, and saw a lady, beckoning them with her hand to come to her. But they ran away. They ran into the village, saying they had seen Our Lady. Their parents were upset, and said it was blasphemy. The children repeated that they did see her. But they could not prove anything. The village was in turmoil. Everybody just waited for the next day.

So, the next day at the same time, 2:00 P.M., everyone came to the hill, and saw the light. All fell on their knees. Some in the thorns. The light vanished and the children saw Our Lady. So Vicka sprinkled holy water on her, and said: "If you are Satan, go away." Our Lady smiled, and said, *Do not be afraid.* They prayed with her, as Vicka's grandmother had told them, the Creed, seven Our Father's, seven Hail Mary's, and seven Glory Be's.

Then Vicka turned around and said, "See, we didn't lie." Everybody believed, except the parents of the children, and me, Fr. Jozo.

Our Lady said to the children: *I have chosen you. I have called you. I need you. You are important to me.* She says those same words to every pilgrim.

Jakov was only a boy of ten, yet she had said to him, *You are important.* You can understand how Abraham was important, how Moses was important. Centuries before Christ, Israel had a great crisis when Saul was king. A giant, Goliath, menaced the armies of Israel. What the king could not do, God could do. He found a boy, David. He said to him, "Do not be afraid. Go, in My name and meet Goliath." Later on, Christ said to the apostles, "Go in My name, heal the sick, raise the dead, drive out devils." And, in His name, they did just that. Likewise, armed in the name of the Lord, David slew Goliath and freed Israel.

David was important. He was important because he had been anointed by the Lord, and had become a prophet who could act in the name of the Lord. You too were anointed at Baptism and Confirmation. Not like warmongers, for God does not give us shot and shell, He gives us no other weapon but His name. The Church fought the Roman Empire for 300 years. Guess what? The one which had all the weapons lost the battle.

How will you overcome nations, the world, renew the Church? By writing a new book? No! By theologizing? No! Our Lady calls us to prayer. Because I know how to pray, I am a prophet. I am a prophet when I speak the word of God, and to God.

Jesus cannot be just a blur in our lives. He is the key, a sign, a sacrament. He gives signs to the Church and is a sign of the Church. There are many untruthful signs which many people follow. The saints never lost the sign. The Church cannot forget the saints. Israel cannot forget Moses. The Church cannot forget Jesus. Our Lady wants to show us Jesus, to give Him back to the people. You have to believe this, to have faith.

Jakov had said to me, "Tomorrow Our Lady will come into the Church."

I answered, "I cannot believe that. Yesterday she came on the hill, then the wineshop, then your house. I cannot believe that."

Jakov replied, "I cannot help you, because you have no faith." I confess to you now, I think about that.

In Nazareth, Jesus could do no works because of their unbelief. I am very repentant and sad about my former doubts. Jakov was right. But I had great opportunity to make amends, through my time in prison when they sentenced me. Jakov was right. That night, at midnight, everyone went home, and waited.

The next day at noon, the church was packed. I saw this. Everybody was waiting for something, like people in a theater waiting for a show to begin. So, I said, "We will pray till

5:30." I gave instructions on the mysteries of the rosary and I was asking God to show us the truth.

"I know You are on the altar," I said, "But I am not sure that Your Mother is on the hill."

At the 5:30 Mass, I told the people that we have the Mass, we don't need revelation. The people would not listen. They wanted witness. I could not give it.

The Bishop came and said the Mass, and gave support to the children. He said, "The children don't lie, they see Our Lady." The people applauded.

Jakov said that he had a message for us. Because he was so short, he asked to be put on the altar. There, he said that Our Lady wanted them to say the rosary. The people applauded again. "Pray the rosary every day, pray together. To pray the rosary, we can get to know Jesus." And so, it had happened.

Our Lady asks for prayer. Believe her, you are also important. The gift of prayer is waiting to be born in you. This is a gift of God. Just as spring touches all trees and causes them to bloom, so prayer is the spring of the Christian life. The body breathes when it is alive; when dead, it doesn't breathe. The soul breathes when it is praying. A Christian who prays is alive. A Christian who does not pray is dead.

Coming to Medjugorje is the spring of your Church. Become a blooming person. Bring a bouquet of flowers to America, be that bouquet, thus beautifying and converting your community.

She also asks us to fast. Not only not to eat; fasting is much deeper. It means to forgive, not to give our spouse the silent treatment; to renounce my plans that are contrary to theirs and militant against true happiness. It is to fast from words that destroy, that bring anger, fast from fashions, sports, etc.

The name of the idol is not important, we all have one. Destroy the idol. Fasting disposes us to do God's will. Our Lady said that Satan is powerful.

What does Our Lady want from Medjugorje? She wants us to find salvation through Jesus. And to find Jesus, through prayer, monthly confession, Scripture, Mass and fasting. All those things we know already. But we stopped. She is teaching us, again.

One day a lady from Vietnam came up to me and told me how it was when she was forced to leave her home during the war. Leaving her home, she turned and gave one last look. She saw the statue of Mary still sitting there. It seemed to say to her, "Don't leave me behind." She went back for it.

Don't leave Mary behind here in Medjugorje. Let her be mother of your family, of your parish, community, nation. Don't forget that the most important thing is to take Our Lady home with you.

She waited 6 years and 11 months for you to come here. She is patient. Be patient with yourself. Let the spirit grow in you gradually. But let it grow.

Fr. Jozo Zovko
Tihaljina, Yugoslavia
May 24, 1988

Chapter VIII
YOU ARE ALL IMPORTANT

(From a talk given to an American pilgrimage, October, 1987)

The people were looking for Jesus. During the night they discovered Him. So from all the cities and neighboring areas they came to listen to Jesus. All day they listened to Him and they were happy. When evening came, Jesus looked at all those people there who had nothing to eat or drink, who had not eaten all day. He was sorry for the people so He turned to His disciples and said:

"Give them something to eat!"

But Peter said, "We do not have anything; You did not tell us—we did not bring any food. After all, even if You had told us, who could bring enough food for so many people?"

Peter used human logic. There was one man there who had been cured by Jesus. He said, "Master, there is here a little boy who did not eat his lunch because he was listening to You." And Jesus asked for the boy to be brought to Him. The man went to the boy and said, "The Teacher is asking for you. He needs your lunch." So what happened? The little boy was obviously excited, the Teacher was asking for his lunch. So he took the whole basket and brought it to Jesus and said to Him, "Here it is, eat." He must have been very honored in this.

In the basket were 5 loaves and 2 fishes. Jesus took them and you can imagine what Jesus' feelings were for the little boy had offered all his lunch to Him. Again, Peter probably thought in a very provoked manner, "What is that for so many

39

people?" Most everyone else probably had the same thought. Only in the eyes of the Lord was that enough. He touched the loaves and the fishes with His hands and blessed them and said to His disciples,

"Distribute this to the people."

The disciples took the food and gave it to all the people. All of them were fed and all of them were satisfied. And there were 12 baskets of leftovers—12 baskets.

Peter had thought there was not enough, but in the hands of the Lord there was enough and more besides. The people felt that the little boy had given all of them his lunch. They all looked at Jesus and the little boy, but they could not understand that what the little boy had given to Jesus, He multiplied to feed the entire crowd. Who can say that this little boy was not important? Who can say, here today, that any sacrifice you make—your gift to Jesus—is not important? Or that Jesus does not need your gift?

The Blessed Mother says, "I need your prayers. Pray the Rosary." When you have the Rosary in your hands, it is not a little thing. The Rosary is composed of five decades. Those five decades are the five loaves in your hands. How is it that you cannot understand that with the Rosary in your hands you can feed other people? The Rosary is important in your hands. The Blessed Mother is looking for you in the same way that Jesus was looking for that little boy. Do not pray just words or just thoughtlessly pray. You must have it in your heart. That is what she wants.

Her last message is almost like the first one:

"And again I am calling you to pray!"

That is not a sign that the Church is not praying. It is a sign that the Church is called to pray. You are called to pray. There is no Church if there is not prayer. We must not say the name of Jesus or announce or proclaim it without it being a prayer.

For that reason every one of you have been blessed. America is waiting for all of you because you are like the prophet Moses who came down from the top of Mt. Sinai. Now you have your call and are going back. Just think about Moses when he came down from Mt. Sinai and he found that the people had built the golden idol. Do you remember that? Can you imagine how strong his prayer must have been to destroy that idol? Every prophet is called to destroy idols and free his people. You must be a prophet. When you go home, do not be afraid to destroy, with joy, all those idols where ever you find them. Maybe even your own hands made some of them in the past. Destroy them with joy.

Think about David. He was a shepherd. Then in front of his parents and his brothers he was anointed to be a king and a prophet. You have heard of Goliath who was going to destroy the people. Saul could not overpower him, nor could the armies do it. But God said to David, "You are going to do it." David was astonished. He said, "This is impossible. How can I do it?"

God said, "In My name you are going to do it. Look in your shepherd's bag and take the five stones you find there."

So David took the stones and his sling. Goliath came out— huge and strong—a warrior, and he laughed. Then he was angry. "Who is this?" he said, "I am looking for a soldier who is going to fight with me." But David said, "I am not here as a soldier, I am here because Yahweh sent me. In God's name I am sent." You all know what happened, Goliath was killed. David became the safeguard of his people.

You are all a prophet. You are all important. Remember, the prophet stops being important when he disobeys. It seems funny when God says to David, "Take the five stones." But David became great because he listened to God. Later, Jesus would explain that what is impossible for man is possible with God. Today, when the Blessed Mother would like to renew the Church, she does not ask money from President Reagan, or bank credit. She did not say, "Go to Geneva and have a conversation with the Russians." She said, "PRAY!"

Would you really believe what could be done with your Rosary in your hands? Or with the stones in the sling of a mere boy? That which you have in your hands is a holy weapon. "Come to Medjugorje" means to believe in God and what he is giving to us, and what the Blessed Mother is giving to us. It is something guaranteed by God, not by some temporal power. Those five stones given to David are also the five decades of the Rosary. I am saying this because you can believe that the Rosary is a weapon secured by God, and you can be assured of this and believe.

Many ask me why the Blessed Mother chose Medjugorje to appear to the six children. Medjugorje is like a desert. There was no water, no facilities. You do not find some contemporary culture or a large historical city there. There is nothing there. And so you have nothing to hold your attention or sway your heart except her. There is nothing else there but Mary.

What are you going to take from Medjugorje? Those people who sell things in those booths, we call gypsies. All of that means nothing. You came here to find the one who has been waiting for you for over six years. Take her back with you. She needs you. You are important to her. And so we finish now with what she is asking from us. Let us pray.

✝   ✝   ✝

Lord we thank You that You have called us from the other side of the world to be here. Thank You for sending Your Mother here. Thank You, Mary, for these many years of your presence. Every day you continue to bring new birth to the Church. Thank you for these new born ones from America today.

Bless them, bless their families, bless their priests, their bishops, the whole Church.

Holy Mother, Blessed Mother, our hearts are open. We are willing and we desire to take you home like the disciple at the foot of the cross. We would like to take you into our homes and our families.

Jesus, we thank You for the gift of Your Mother. You gave her to the disciple who loved You. So we, too, desire to love You. Give us Your love and give it also to those who do not know how to love. Touch our hearts, dear Jesus, and heal us. Open Your hands for us. Bless us, protect us, bless all those who are suffering. Bless our needs, our troubles, and our sufferings. Bless all those who are infirm and sick; bring your peace and blessing forever. In the name of the Father, and the Son, and the Holy Spirit. Amen.''

Fr. Jozo Zovko
Tihaljina, Yugoslavia
October 3, 1987

Crowd Gathering For Evening Mass.

Chapter IX
CONVERSION—OUR FIAT

(A talk given May 12, 1989, to American Peace Center pilgrims.)

I would like to tell you right at the beginning that you made no mistake in deciding to come over here to this country. You have made one big step. Even after you had your tickets, there still were many temptations and reasons why perhaps you need not come. That is why Our Lady isn't satisfied with any pilgrim from the moment of leaving the house until they arrive here. Satan was not pleased with your decision to come over here and was causing all these temptations.

Surely, from the moment when you left your house there were so many temptations. But surely Satan is pleased with those who, after leaving Medjugorje and going back home, have remained closed and unchanged.

I want your pilgrimage truly to be a meeting with God, and I want you to give your answer to Our Lady.

I don't want to give you just all kinds of information. I only want to stand by the side of the road, as we meet for a moment on your journey, to tell you that you did not make a mistake in coming here, and to help you and show you the way to continue further on.

To me, every pilgrim who comes to Medjugorje is like a river. Rivers flow from all directions; they do not start from the same place. The thing they have in common is that they are all flowing towards the ocean where they are going to be mixed together with the ocean water.

All water flowing into the ocean is giving up its old exis-

44

tence, but it doesn't cease existing. It continues to exist, but now, being mixed together with the ocean, it continues in its new existence. The many smaller rivers are all mixed together with the much larger ocean.

The pilgrim coming to Medjugorje is also mixed together with the ocean, but this time it is the ocean of prayer. Pilgrims who are open as they come here to Medjugorje, become one with Medjugorje—they become mixed together with the spirituality of Medjugorje.

Pilgrims coming to Medjugorje meet the parish that is fasting, and they immediately are inspired to start to fast, as well as to make sacrifices and do penance, realizing the significance, the meaning and the value of fasting and sacrifice.

Water is open, free, and at the disposal of all. The open water of the ocean accepts the water flowing into it and it becomes mixed together as one water.

Now imagine a tightly closed bottle floating on the water of the ocean. The sealed bottle doesn't take anything from the ocean and doesn't give anything to the ocean.

That is why Our Lady, as the first step, opened the parishioners of Medjugorje and now tries to do the same with every pilgrim who comes.

That is why everyone feels welcome in Medjugorje. In Medjugorje, no one feels like a stranger, as a foreigner.

There was a small Orthodox community that left here just before you came. They have been here many times, and every time they come to Medjugorje, they go to confession. They don't do that anywhere else, but in Medjugorje these things happen.

A Protestant pastor brought his daughter here for her first Holy Communion, a convert. The whole family celebrated together with us for that celebration.

An Anglican bishop took part in the adoration of the Most Blessed Sacrament here in Medjugorje. That happens nowhere else in other churches of the world, but it happens here in Medjugorje.

Also, most every day in Medjugorje there are Muslim people who come and, mixed together with the people of the parish and other pilgrims, pray with them in the church.

No one is organizing pilgrimages for these people. It is only Our Lady who invited them. Everyone who comes to Medjugorje feels that Heaven is speaking directly to them.

Medjugorje is such a small place that you can't find it on the maps of Yugoslavia. Yet, you all succeeded to find this little place. Why is that? It is because our Mother is here. And we have all heard the voice of our Mother, and we all recognize her voice and her call.

Medjugorje is the voice of our heavenly Mother, the voice that everyone hears in one's proper time.

Imagine the noises that have existed for such a long time, which were covering this voice and disabling us from hearing it.

But, yet, her voice reached you, and you recognized her voice, and immediately you knew that it was your Mother talking to you.

I think of Medjugorje as the pool of Siloe in Israel. (*John* 9:7) That pool of water became the place of hope for so many sick people in Israel. Medicine could not heal the people, but the water, moved by the hand of an angel, could heal. It was a place where many sick people gathered, a place of hope as everyone was hoping to be the one who would be healed. It was very natural (It was the thing to do) to go and visit that place.

And this is how Jesus went there. He wasn't looking for the water, but He was looking at His Father and at Himself. And then Jesus healed the blind man who had been waiting by the waters for many years.

Medjugorje is that same water of Siloe. It is the hand of Our Lady that has moved the miraculous water in this pool for the last eight years. It doesn't matter what kind of sickness you have brought in coming. It doesn't matter what sickness. The point is not whether you are going to die.

Our Lady says, "Don't be afraid. It is me. Everyone can be healed."

And it is now your turn. Imagine how beautiful you will be when healed completely; when you go back home healed!

Healthy in your heart, in your body, in your soul. Healed from any evil.

You came as a river flowing into the ocean of Medjugorje. Being purified here, you are going back home, still as a river, but this time your water is as clear as spring water, as pure as Holy Water.

I think of the millions of pilgrims who have found this healing. Medjugorje for us is really our Siloe.

(The Lord's Prayer and other prayers were recited by the congregation at this point.)

I see Medjugorje as the embracement of me, a rakish son, with my good loving Father.

Medjugorje for me, also, is like a big table that has been prepared for the family feast. And no one is sitting in someone else's chair. Everyone recognizes their own place. Everyone found one's own chair of conversion. One's own place and position of renouncement and sacrifice and love is waiting for each of us.

It is then so easy to consume this miraculous bread of prayer that is nourishing us with peace and love and joy.

This feast has been going on for the last eight years, and there is a place for everyone. And from my place I can see all my brothers and sisters. I am so glad and pleased to see that your chairs are now occupied, and that you will get your part in the feast. Therefore, I say, "Welcome."

I would like to tell you a little bit about Medjugorje and my own experience—not in order to give you new data and information, but to help you find peace, that you may find yourself as well.

I would like to begin by assuring you of how important you are, and this I will do by telling you one little story.

A man, contemplating his own importance before God and significance in God's plan, wrote the following meditation. He said:

"One day, it was raining while I was in my room.
It rained after many dry months. And I saw the
first drop of rain fall on the road causing a little

bit of mud out of the dust on the road. Another drop fell on the red iron in the blacksmith shop across from my house. In touching the red iron, the drop of rain vaporized. One drop fell on the rose before my window, and as I was watching, I could see the rose opening its little head and drinking that drop of water, turning it later into life.

One drop of rain fell in an open shell on the bank of the river. The shell closed itself, and after some time it turned the drop of rain into a beautiful pearl.

All of these drops fell from the same cloud, and they were all the same. But they ended in different ways. And their end did not depend on them, but on the place on which they fell."

What is going to happen on your pilgrimage depends only on you.

I am telling you this because I would like this pilgrimage to be turned into a part of your life. I wish that you go back home as a really rich person. I want you to go back home together with the pearl you have found in Medjugorje; with the treasury Our Lady wants to give to every one of you as her beloved children.

It is what she wants, but it doesn't depend on her. You must desire that too. And this program (my talk with you) is only to be a contribution to that, and nothing more.

You should desire nothing less than that this pilgrimage become a pearl of your life, something according to which you will be different from other people.

And how are you going to obtain that? First, what Our Lady wants of us in Medjugorje is to be open as the shell was on the river bank. We know how to open a bottle; how to unlock a door. (Doors are big, but see how little the key is. The little key is used for opening the big door.) I want you to imagine the little key as being a good deed that you can perform which can open such big doors. Our Lady asks you to be inwardly open.

The visionary, Maria, a young girl, was coming down the

hill of Podbrdo bringing us the message of conversion. Hearing that child's voice, adults' hearts were opened. But I was confused for I didn't know what that meant. This is now my confession to you, and it is always a serious moment for me.

In the beginning, I had preached all week on the subject of conversion, and, in my opinion, these sermons were very good. Yet, I didn't convert anyone. How then could they be good sermons when they didn't convert anyone? If the seed sowed didn't sprout, then we can't say that the seeds were good. But that was really the right thing to happen. Our Lady was right; Our Lady is always right. She let me talk about conversion throughout the whole week, and didn't let anyone convert.

Our Lady then came and helped us. She helped us to make this first step as a little child would make its first step. Then Our Lady invited us on our next step, and that step is called prayer.

And now, after eight years, when I think about those first steps, I realize how important and significant they were. And every person in the parish took those first steps. And now I will explain to you how it happened with us.

Policemen were blocking the area and trying to keep the children from coming to church. The children were closed up in their houses. But days are long and the children would spend the time in their houses thinking of how they will break through that wall of policemen around their houses, and they always managed to find a way.

It was a hot summer. A poor policeman might spend all night keeping watch over the house, and then after the long night, during the hot summer day, he might drop off to sleep for just a moment and the children would use the opportunity to jump through a window of their house and continue their run towards the church.

One particular day, little Jakov changed cars six times in order to come to church (since they were checking all cars on the roads). He arrived at the church just at the moment I was ending the Mass. As I bent to kiss the altar, someone pulled on my sleeve. I looked down and it was Jakov. He was motioning to me that he had something to tell me. As I put my head next to his, he whispered in my ear that he had an important message for the people.

I put him on the altar before the microphone, and he said, "Our Lady says to pray the rosary every day and to pray together." They applauded.

As I looked at the people in the church, I saw all of them crying. They all understood the voice and the message of Our Lady. They all heard and recognized in these words the voice of their Mother—All except me.

Really, it is sad but it is true. I was standing on the left of the altar, and I was looking at little Jakov when he gave that announcement, but I didn't believe him. I wondered and I asked myself, "What did these people hear!? These are such simple words and yet they are all crying!"

Spontaneously, everyone's hand went into their pockets and they took out their rosaries. And the people said, "Let's pray."

I said, "Bravo! I, too, am for prayer." And so we started to pray. And, as we prayed all night long, Our Lady appeared in the church. Our Lady appeared in the middle of the church, in the very heart of the church, as a mother would appear among her children. We stopped our prayer and we greeted her with one beautiful song. Our Lady repeated the same message that little Jakov said to the people after the Mass.

And I know and I am convinced that she did not appear in the church and give that message because of the people in the church, for they already believed; and not because of the visionaries, because they believed too. But I know that she appeared because of me, because she wanted me to believe.

And since that moment, since that day, I believe all the children: Jakov, Ivanka, Vicka, Ivan, Mirjana, Maria.

It is interesting what Our Lady added to her message that evening. She said, "Thank you for having responded to my call."

These words explained immediately the depths of the words

Our Lady said previously: "I have invited you . . . You are important to me. . .I have chosen you. . .I have called you." The one who responds to her call becomes important, therefore, she says to them, "Thank you for having responded to my call."

I thank you for coming. And, in the name of Our Lady, thank you for responding to her message. And this is the message today which is placed before you: Pray the rosary every day and pray together.

Since that day, the parish church in Medjugorje has never missed one single day to pray the rosary. And there were some hard days. The Bishop and the Provincial superior of the Franciscans were replacing the priests. Also, the Communist political authorities were replacing priests. All of them had taken on the right to change them. But no one dared to say that we could not pray. The message of Our Lady remains to this day.

Why pray? Why the prayer of the rosary?

The rosary is a biography. It is the story of the life of Jesus. It is the story of the life of the Blessed Virgin Mary. And it is the history of the Church.

To pray the rosary means to contemplate the mysteries of the life of Jesus and Mary, and it means at the same time truly to know Jesus. To pray the rosary means to receive grace, to fall in love with Jesus, as well as to receive strength to inherit Jesus—to live as Jesus.

There are people who try to know Jesus by studying. But to study theology, to study some science has only intellectual value. But to love Jesus is another grace. It is a gift of love.

One cannot love Jesus unless he prays. And he who doesn't pray, doesn't know Jesus. Our life is a grace, it is our grace. And no one has recognized and comprehended Jesus or found Jesus in the same way as we do as we go along our path, a path along which the Holy Spirit is inspiring us.

As the Bible says, it is the Holy Spirit that is praying within us. Our prayers should be in union with the Holy Spirit. In fact, our prayers are being born out of the Holy Spirit.

Some people pray as beggars; they pray only for their needs. But they are just reciting words. They are praying out of their human needs. But a Christian is the only one that prays out of the Holy Spirit.

Therefore, Our Lady says that by prayer we can accomplish everything.

In church this morning, there was a customs officer. I had formerly baptized him and his whole family. He now has grown children, and they were married then in the Church.

Today he is living the life of an apostle of Jesus in Medjugorje. He had addressed a group of Italian pilgrims in church this morning. He talked openly to them; he even mentioned the abortion his wife had. He told them that his parents were Communists, atheists. And when his wife went to the hospital for the abortion, they all agreed. No one said that what they were doing was wrong, not colleagues, people he works with, people she works with, nor family and friends. And this is what is upsetting to him now, that there was no one, no one to say how wrong they were then.

So, now his intention is this: To teach children, young people and others who have never before heard the word of Jesus. And to take the place of their parents, teachers and others who should teach them about God.

He converted his apartment, his home, into a little chapel. He is totally convinced that through prayer and by prayer one can accomplish everything.

This is the experience of Medjugorje.

You are in Medjugorje. You have come to that pool of miraculous water which can heal you from all which our modern generation is suffering.

But there is something else that I would like to tell you in order to help you recognize what Our Lady wants from us. The first step along the path of conversion on which Our Lady invited us was (as we have already heard) prayer, prayer with the heart, daily praying of the rosary. The second step along this path of conversion is fasting.

Our Lady says fast. And it is good fortune that Our Lady

gave this message to a parish that was welcoming her messages with so much enthusiasm.

All the world thinks that American people (known in the world as rich people) are fasting so little. So it will be an interesting healing now when you go back home and say to your neighbors, friends and relatives, "Today is a Friday and I fast."

To fast does not mean only not to eat, but fasting is freedom—a freedom that is needed badly by us all. You might say, "Today is Friday; I want to be free, free from cigarettes."

To be free is something that we are all looking for. Very often we say, "He's addicted to drugs or to alcohol." We are wrong if we call only people that are addicted to drugs and alcohol "addicts" when there are so many who are addicted to cigarettes, to their weekends, to TV programs and movies, to so many things. Every kind of addiction is bondage. So one can fast by deciding to switch off the TV.

Fasting can be done also with our eyes by deliberately trying to meet and see everyone with love. Fasting means "changing us." Fasting is freeing us from the mask of egotism. Only one who loves can fast. Fasting is sacrifice. Fasting is love.

I will never be able to comprehend the cross of Jesus as the supreme mystery of love, unless I start to fast. Fasting is important to us being Adam's childen.

It was a Wednesday when Our Lady invited us to begin fasting. Now we know that she helped us with one significant step along the path of conversion. When people heard that she said to fast, they were full of enthusiasm. On the third day of fasting, the people had but one desire and that was to confess. There were over 100 priests hearing confession. Our sleeves were wet from tears. We were touched by every confession. And that same day Our Lady invited us to monthly confesssion.

We priests who were hearing confessions that day in Medjugorje, being priests from different areas, for the first time in our priesthood we could comprehend the real depth of that Holy Sacrament of Confession. People were eagerly destroying their idols, and going back home freed. We strongly felt that confession means to destroy one's own idols, and that it means to put Jesus in the first place in our lives.

Since then, the parishioners have been going to confession on the first weekend of the month, a weekend of reconciliation. And most pilgrims who come to Medjugorje try, from then on, to continue with the same practice.

Only a few of the priests in this area speak English. I am sad that I don't speak English. When we went to school, we thought that the United States was so far from our country that we would never see an American in our life. We learned German, French, Italian, Russian. And now we are sad that we don't speak English. I can't hear your confession, but I can celebrate Mass for you.

It is an interesting experience for all of us here in Medjugorje that languages are not separating us, but that there is another language, a language that is uniting us all and that we all understand well. It is the language of prayer.

Our Lady cried in Medjugorje. And, believe me, it is not pleasant at all to talk about it. It is sad. But as you are a pilgrim and my brother, I would like with all my heart to tell you something about it.

Our Lady cried when she talked about priests. She said, "To my dear sons, tell them to have firm faith. Tell them to keep the faith of my people and have compassion for them."

To say that to her beloved sons means we must pray for her priests.

She would also cry when she talked about the Eucharist. It is a sacrifice, a sacrifice for all, a gift of Heaven to all. The altar in your parish church is the same as this altar, and every altar presents the opened and extended hands of the priests who are offering the Supreme, the Most Precious Gift, Jesus Himself. It is Jesus then Who says, "Come and take of My body and eat all."

The tabernacle has been keeping our God Emmanuel among us for almost 2,000 years. Next to the tabernacle there is an eternal light, the same light that Moses saw on Sinai. And he heard out of that light the voice of Yahweh. And it is there that he heard about his mission to go to Egypt and free the people. It is of great happiness for God, as well as for the Israeli people, that Moses was a humble and obedient prophet. Every Mass is sending us as prophets.

Jesus lighted that eternal light at the Last Supper. And it is the Church that keeps that light burning even until today.

I don't know what tabernacle means to you. I do not know what altar means to you. I do not know what Sunday morning Mass at your parish means to you. But I know that Our Lady, with her tears, wants to open and purify your eyes and enable you to recognize what it is that Jesus wants from us.

Our Lady cries also when she talks about the Bible. And she talks about it in a simple way. She says, "You have forgotten the Bible."

This has been impregnated deeply in my mind, and every time when I think of that message I recall the picture of the first station of the Way of the Cross—Jesus before the priests and Pilate. His people betrayed Him by choosing to vote against Him. The Israeli people chose wrong. Every generation chooses; every one of us individually chooses.

Our Lady cries telling us that we have chosen wrong; that we haven't chosen the Bible. We have accepted mountains of different newspapers and magazines. (I can just imagine how many there are in the United States.) We have chosen and accepted to spend hours and hours before the television. We have chosen our own words, human words, an abundance of human words—and we have forgotten the Word of God.

To come to Medjugorje means to rediscover the Bible, to start to live the Bible and to listen well to what it reveals, what this Divine Word has done in the heart and in the life of Our Lady. The embodiment of the New Testament, the Words of Our Lord, is always current, always alive. The Word of God with that same power and strength is waiting for your fiat, just as Mary gave hers.

What joy and happiness echoed in the hearts of us, in the heart of the Church, and particularly in the hearts of the millions of people in Soviet Union with the news that the Bible is coming back to the Soviet Union. In Stockholm, Sweden, the Minister of Culture and Education of the Soviet Union has signed documents according to which the government of Sweden will give 50 million copies of the Bible as a present to Soviet Union's people. That is sensational in this century; a great gift, grace and miracle that this could happen!

Imagine, many years ago people were sentenced to jail because of the Bible. You had good fortune if you didn't lose your job, lose your right to an education or be imprisoned because of your faith, because of the Bible.

But you could choose. You were always free to choose. How have you chosen? All I want to say to you is: Choose the Bible. Read the Bible together with your children. Let this Divine Word of God dwell again within the walls of your houses. And after every reading, before closing the Bible, kiss it. And when your son or daughter ask you why did you kiss it, explain to them. Tell them that you kiss the Bible because you love Jesus. Tell them, "It was Jesus whose voice we just listened to; Who spoke to us. And I love Him. I kiss Him."

Our Lady doesn't ask from us what is impossible to realize and accomplish. But she is calling us all because we are the Church. Without all of us, the Church cannot exist.

She is, therefore, calling us back to what we have forgotten. Prayer in the family every day; prayer with the heart. Not as a beggar reciting words, but as a Christian with the Holy Spirit praying in your heart. Fasting, penance, peace, reconciliation, Eucharist and the Bible. These are foundation stones for the building Our Lady has been constructing. And the building she is building is called our conversion. This is how Our Lady is preparing us, as the Church, for the third millenium Church that will be full of light.

Don't be afraid. You have come to the pool of Siloe, the pool of healing.

Close your eyes and let us pray.

> *Lord, with your Divine Hands, take these pictures and scapulars and let them become the visible signs of Your and Your Mother's presence. Take all*

rosaries in Your Hands and bless them as well. We are responsible to you and to the Church for our pilgrimage. Speak to us. Teach us. Change us. Heal us. We really want to take a new step in our life. We want to take back home with us the messages of Our Lady, and we want to live them. But this is something that we cannot do without Your blessing.

Therefore, our heart is open. Give us Your blessing. Heal the sick ones. Open our blind eyes and let us see what we couldn't see. Let us love what we didn't love. Let us all go back home to our families as prophets full of joy. Let us all go back home with a clear task and aim, to renew the Church, to renew the faith, to love.

Oh, God, I depend on You. Let Your grace fill us all. Let Your grace fill our hearts. And let healing take place in us.

Oh, Mother, here we are, your beloved children. We all need you. And you are important to us. We have heard your voice. We want to give you our answer. Help us. Comfort all the hearts that are sad. Heal the sick ones and strengthen us all, protect us all and come back home with us and be Mother to us all and be our comforter.

Jesus, Your blessing is the help we seek. It is the blessing we need. Bless us with Your cross, and with Your cross, bless our crosses and our sacrifices and sufferings. Let our cross become our salvation and our peace.

Bless us, dear Jesus, in the name of the Father, and of the Son, and of the Holy Spirit. Amen.

Fr. Jozo Zovko
Tihaljina, Yugoslavia
May 12, 1989

Chapter X
SIX YEARS

(A talk to American pilgrims given on June 25, 1987.)

The tree that has been growing these past six years is bearing fruit in abundance. Its branches have spread wide. Our Lady has been calling the Church to pray, and we feel as if the Church is awakening. This Marian Year, which the Pope proclaimed, is allowing us to recognize the fruits of the apparitions. The Pope called the whole Church to awaken to the third millennium of Christianity, the wish to place Our Lady in the center of the Church as a mother, as a teacher of prayer.

Jesus did not learn to pray in the temple. Jesus was not taught prayer by a rabbi. He didn't learn to pray in synagogues. Jesus learned how to pray from his family; he was taught how to pray by His mother. Our Lady is an educator and a tutor. But she calls us dear children, not dear students, and she wants to awaken us softly through prayer.

Through her calls to conversion and penance these past six years, we see daily that many of those who have been away from the Church are returning to it. Those who left her are coming back again. Those who have remained as childen of God and become nervous because of these apparitions, she is comforting, asking why they are upset if people are converting and going to confession and are coming back again. She is saying to every bishop and every priest to be glad and rejoice! This is the day we should celebrate; this is the day of the banquet. Our Lady is celebrating the victory over the enemy of the Church, the enemy of our peace and our salvation.

It is the fruits of the many conversions that we recognize here in Medjugorje; the conversions of our human hearts, the grace of conversion and changes in us who were wounded by selfishness.

Then there are other fruits which are recognized—the readiness of people to live the message of peace. I remember when we saw the word MIR (peace) written in big, burning letters in the sky over the cross on Mt. Krizevac. We were shocked. The moments passed, but we were unable to speak. No one dared say a word. Slowly, we came to our senses. We realized that we were still alive. We started to comment and talk about what we had experienced. The word MIR was blazing in the sky, but the same word was written in our hearts. I felt that there was not a person present who didn't want to live that peace. I felt that there was not a person present in whose heart God was unable to inscribe the desire for peace, and in whose heart God was not able to open the spring from which barren grounds would be watered.

After that, there wasn't a person who was not peaceful. There wasn't a family that lived in unrest. You see, that is very important that people began to want peace—to make peace and to live peace. This is a fruit which cannot be produced by men of politics, by men of arms, by means of force. Only the Son of God can give peace and with it nourish the Church and the entire world.

This is felt in Medjugorje in prayer, in life with the Church through the sacraments, life with the Bible, learning the Word of God and living it. Our Lady said, "You have forgotten the Bible. You have forgotten the Word of my Son, you have forgotten the Word of God." She started to cry. Our Lady explained why. The Bible was missing in many families—even those families that called themselves Christians. It is impossible to pray if one does not read and listen to God's word. Jesus said, "He who listens to my word, who places it in his heart and lives it, he is my brother and my sister and my mother."

Fruits are visible, they are being lived, they are being offered to the world not only to come to Medjugorje, but to become Medjugorje. The Church came alive in Medjugorje like a seed. And this seed carries within it all the essentials for life, the main characteristics of a tree which will grow. This is a great fruit, a great gift and great grace that has been visible here through these six years—the life and presence of Our Lady in Medjugorje.

Our Lady would not have been able to express herself fully if she had only left the word MIR in the sky along with other visible signs. There would be something left out and everyone would imagine different things. She reached out for something concrete. She found for herself those of the village who are the most simple, those whom other people would probably never choose. But she, as a mother, chose just those—the little ones, the seers.

I remember how determined and inflexible they were in the first days. I remember how they made me lose sleep at night and I had no peace. They even made me feel inadequate. I found it difficult to believe the children. I was afraid that people might ridicule the Church. I couldn't believe that the children could have a conversation with Our Lady. Their parents did not believe them and I didn't believe them. But they believed within themselves and they kept repeating the same things every day.

Then the persecutions began, but the children endured. I remember when they came running from the police. I was in the church by myself praying. I was saddened by the behavior of my parishioners who left the church to go to the apparition mountain. I began to pray very sincerely for I was very troubled. "Lord, what if the people going to the mountain are really offending You. You gave signs to Moses on how to lead his people. I want to be on Your side; I don't want these people to be deceived here."

Then I heard a voice while I was praying; it said to me, "Go out and protect the children." I was in the third pew on the right. Our Lady's statue stood before me. Without a second thought, I got up and walked out. The children were running from the left side, out of breath, frightened, and swarmed around me like bees and said, "Protect us; the police are after us." I took them into a room in the rectory and locked the door. I went outside and sat under a tree, and the police came running up and asked, "Did you see the children?" I said, "Yes." And they kept running in the direction of the village where the children are from. That day was the first time the children had the apparition in the rectory.

It was the next evening after the Mass that Our Lady came to the church. Until that day, I did not believe. Our Lady came and made herself known to us, so when I actually received the grace, thanks to God and Our Lady, I started to listen over and over again to the tapes on which everything was recorded from the first day. I listened to the words of the children, and they now seemed to have a different meaning. I listened to those same words of the children, but with much hope, certainly and beauty. Before, every word had caused unrest in me, uncertainty. But the children were stubborn and knew how to suffer for the truth, and later became great apostles, apostles whom Our Lady used, through their meekness and weaknesses, to proclaim the great name of Jesus and to distribute great gifts.

These children were not extensively educated in the faith but were just like anyone else in the village, children who were not outstanding in any way. But now they live the kind of life that even some of the clergy would find difficult.

The seers became witnesses. They became instruments— the first to begin to live the messages. They lived the faith that Our Lady taught them. No one today is going through what they are going through. They listen to so many problems, weaknesses and illnesses of other people. And they always appear peaceful and happy. The seers are a great sign—especially for us priests—of how we should be patient in dealing with the weaknesses of our people, to accept them and to keep presenting them to God. The seers themselves are a great sign that Our Lady lifts up for all to see, in order to realize her plans.

(Fr. Jozo was asked, "How are we to pray?")

When Jesus wanted to teach us how to pray, He first said how **not** to pray. He warned us not to pray like the Pharisees, just for others to see. Do not just pray for what you are going to wear, eat or drink. Do not place those values first. God knows that you need these things. You should seek first the Kingdom of God.

Our Lady's message the other week said that we should seek the will of our Father. What does this mean, the will of our Father? What does Jesus mean when He says, "My nourishment is to perform the will of the Father?" What does Jesus mean when He says, "Not mine, but Your will be done?"

The first person who knew how to say, "Yes, Father, let it be done as You want," was Our Lady. The second person was her Son, the Son of God, who was constantly declaring this with His life. Jesus inserted this prayer into the "Our Father" when His apostles asked Him to teach them to pray. Jesus said, "Gladly, I will teach you to pray. When you pray, say it this way, feel it this way, think in this way: Our Father, Who art in heaven, hallowed be Your name, etc." But He couldn't omit, ". . .Your will be done. . ."

It seems to me that this is very important, for this is our relationship with God. We are His children, even if we are sinful, we are the children against whom the Father holds nothing when we decide to come home. He always has open arms, an open heart. He keeps prepared a new robe for us, a new ring, a new banquet. This is what happens in the encounter with the Father. So, how should we pray? We should pray as Jesus did—continually.

I have been asked if Medjugorje will undergo much suffering. Yes. Medjugorje is carrying the fate of the Gospel. It is the renewal of the Church. Every renewal means letting go of something that is worn out or becomes too small; but sometimes through fear, we don't want to let go and we can't let go without experiencing pain. It, therefore, seems to me that we are like the crippled man unable to fold up our mat and walk home. We have to leave our past life, as Our Lady told us, and accept and begin a new one. Medjugorje still has to suffer in its confrontation with evil, with dark forces which are hidden in each person and in the Church as well.

Medjugorje does not ask that the Church suffer in that way, but the Church cannot change otherwise. It has to go through pain, through a cleansing fire. You see, when the persecutions of Medjugorje began, the parish started to wake up and feel its responsibility—its responsiblity toward its pastor. After I returned from prison, the faithful told me, "For the first time, we felt we had to pray for this priest that was sent to us, who was granted to us as a gift from God, who is our leader, our teacher. We are responsible for his life. He needs us; we need him."

But these persecutions and sufferings are harder when misunderstandings come from the Church itself. Medjugorje is suffering more because of a misunderstanding from the view of the bishop and the priests who do not recognize the tree of Medjugorje by its fruits, the presence of their God, the presence of Our Lady, their Church and the graces of God. It is here we perhaps feel more sadness. But at the same time, this is a way of our cleansing. This kind of suffering is much greater than when some atheist says, "I want to destroy your faith; I want to destroy your life." The Church is then happy to be able to offer a witnessing for Christ. When she feels misunderstood by her own, then she feels sad.

Thus, these persecutions and misunderstandings by the Church itself are often an invitation to us, to which we were called by Pope John XXIII, to be able to read and understand the signs of the times.

Medjugorje is a sign for our times, our generation, that our generation becomes what God wants—and this is the Church, the seed, the light, the teacher, the mother, peace, salvation for all, prophet to all, priest and preacher to all. The Church is the servant of the Lord, protector and announcer of the Gospel; but this, unfortunately, we are not always able to do when we are not able to die or suffer, when we are not able to deny ourselves, and when we live instead of having God live within us.

Our Lady is calling, "Leave your past life here." And three

months ago she said, "Put God first in your lives and first in your love." You see, this is more than a war with ourselves, this is more than a call for renewal. It is a reconstruction of our lives. We begin to question our own values. We begin to look inside ourselves as a creator of false gods, false hopes, false securities, false values. And the Church is the one that should free us from this. This is why Medjugorje has to suffer while proclaiming what Our Lady asks of us.

Fr. Jozo Zovko
Tihaljina, Yugoslavia
June 25, 1987

Chapter 11

1989 EASTER VIGIL MASS AT ST. ELIJAH

(A homily by Fr. Jozo, March 25, 1989.)

It is my pleasure tonight to greet our guests, our brothers and sisters from America, who are going to join us in the start of this summer's celebration—100 year anniversary of our parish.

But this celebration is not going to sidetrack the thought which is a central one tonight in the whole Church and in our hearts—Jesus resurrected. God is alive! God, Who follows His Church in every way, is showing to every heart that where God is glorified, where God is loved, where one meets with God, there is His Church, there is His brother, His sister, His family and His treasure.

It is now 7 years, 9 months and 1 day since Our Lady started appearing in Medjugorje, and so many people have come here. When we hear negative stories about these happenings, what can we say? The heart that does not sing the song of the resurrection has not understood Our Lady, who for over seven years has been teaching people to live Easter. She teaches the people that God is alive! She teaches the people as Jesus taught the women at the tomb, "Do not look for me among the dead; I am alive. . ."

Brothers and sisters, our God is alive! This night wants to tell all of us of the joyful song: "Jesus died so that we can live." Jesus' tomb is empty, for life cannot be killed. Life is stronger than death; love is stronger than death.

Through every one of our hearts tonight, Jesus wants to

sing a hymn of life. He wants to touch your heart so that it becomes a temple in which God will be glorified. I would like you to remember this night, this gospel, this divine song through which this choir wants to present to us the resurrection of Jesus.

May this Easter be joyful for all of us. May each one of us come together with our Christian life, our Christian song, our hymn of praise. May each one of us become a witness to the resurrection of Jesus. His tomb called all of those who loved Him, the women and the apostles. They all came and believed. They had already met up with Him on the way. They all discovered that Jesus is alive, and they had become witnesses of the resurrection. Each time one comes to Mass, he is witnessing to the Living God! "My God is alive. I am not afraid to go into the tomb—as Peter did. I am not afraid to go there where the soldiers are keeping guard. I am not afraid to go where I could be killed." Nothing and no one can separate us from the love of Jesus Christ.

When Turkish power was at its peak, the Turks had conquered most of Croatia. They came near Vienna and were advancing to the heart of Europe. It seemed that nothing could stop them. When all else failed, the people went to the churches and began to pray. At one point, something unexpected happened: the news came that the sultan, the Turkish leader, was dead. The soldiers and the guards came into the filled churches and proclaimed, "We are saved!" The bells started ringing and hearts began singing songs of thanksgiving to God. "God saved us!" they sang.

Tonight a messenger from Heaven—an angel of God—is coming into our hearts, into the temple of our love and our faith, and says, "We are saved, brothers and sisters, we are saved!" Jesus freed His people, Jesus died for His people, and we are saved. Tonight, Heaven and earth are proclaiming this joyful news, and the Church is proclaiming the same.

Therefore, let us celebrate this holiday of joy; let us celebrate this holiday of freedom—freedom from evil and freedom from death. May each one of you cross your own "red sea"; may each one of you come from slavery to freedom; may each one of you resurrect as a new person, a new person in the image of God's creation.

Fr. Jozo Zovko
Tihaljina, Yugoslavia
March 25, 1989

Father Jozo.

OBRAĆENJE

(Conversion)

Of the many charisms and insights Father Jozo presents to his many visitors, the meaning of that word "obraćenje" (conversion) is perhaps one of the most extraordinary. He seems to be able to express it in the simplest, yet most compelling ways. It is a difficult and often mis-understood word in our times.

Every time the seers are asked about the "main message" of Our Lady their answers may vary in wording but their meaning is always the same. In the words of Maria: "All the messages concern the world, such as conversion, faith, peace, prayer, and fasting and penance."

Conversion, then, is a basic message from Medjugorje, and conversion is a basic message in all prophecy. Mary, as a special prophet of our time, calls and encourages all people to conversion. Earlier, Jeremiah also called his people to conversion, telling them: "Cleanse your heart of evil." (*Jer.* 4:14). Cleansing your heart of evil is conversion, and Our Lady conveys that power of conversion from God to all peoples, to every person. It is not a message of fear or doom, but God's loving plan and desire to bring each person into His Kingdom. Thus Our Lady has become a prophetess for our time, a time which has lost touch with itself and with God. She wants to put us in touch again. Therefore she has come to Medjugorje, and to the world. That word, "conversion," is the process she requests.

The uncleansed heart is the source of all our evil. Even in Ezekiel's time this judgment was rendered, for He told His people: "As I live, says the Lord God, I swear I take no plea-

68

sure in the death of the wicked man, but in the wicked man's conversion, that he may live." (*Ez.* 33:10-11). How complicated we have made those words.

Today, theologians provide endless volumes of material trying to unravel the mysteries of The Christ, His Church, His words, our salvation. In the process, we wind up trying to re-write the Gospels, modernize the Church and update the Commandments, all in an attempt to layout "the correct means" of our salvation.

So it is with the word "conversion." Our self-appointed intellectualism of today trys to find new meaning, new processes, new ways of adaptation to incorporate conversion into our already complicated lives, and to our detriment.

Father Jozo, on the other hand, reduces it to its simplest and purest terms in conveying the requests of Our Lady to her childen. But as we drink in his thoughts, we suddenly become aware that it has all been said before. It has always been there. Father Jozo, as an instrument of Our Lord and Our Lady, simply brings out those basic truths, those same teachings which have somehow become clouded and obscure in a world too complicated for simple truths.

He points out that the means of conversion are the Eucharist, prayer, penance, fasting, and monthly confession. In response to Our Lady's call for conversion, many people have now resumed daily praying, fasting and various forms of penance; and long lines of penitent pilgrims have re-discovered the Sacrament of Reconciliation in Medjugorje. Fr. Jozo states:

"It is prayer that Our Lady wants of us. The gift of prayer— (for it is a special gift of God)—is waiting to be born in you. Our Lady wants us to find salvation through Jesus. And we find Jesus through prayer, monthly confession, the Scriptures, Mass, and fasting. All these things were already known to us, but we had stopped putting them into proper practice."

In one of his talks to pilgrims Fr. Jozo stated:

"Our Lady explained that to convert means to sacrifice with joy, with love. She said, 'Today may everyone find in his heart all of his enemies and may he show them to his Father with joy. May he pray for them.' She told us to bring fasting and prayer back into our homes, and that she needs each one of us. She said, 'I need your prayer. I need you. You are important. Convert!'

"I finally understood it all. She was talking to me. She is talking to you. She was telling me, 'I want you to convert. Why are you trying to convert everyone else?' She does not say convert your family, your friends, your parishioners. Conversion is not adopting a certain religion. It is a process for each of us individually. Peace begins within you. Love begins within you. Conversion begins within you and the world will never have these things until each of us individually find this change of heart within ourselves. It is for each person. One at a time.

"This world doesn't need our selfishness, but our faith. This world doesn't need our pride, but our love. That is why the Church is a visible sign of the presence of God among people. Let us renew the Church! You are invited! Do not be afraid to answer the call. The one who invited you, works with you . . . it is your God, who will not leave you. It is your mother, who leads you and brings you along. Stay obedient."

As you read some of the talks of Father Jozo in this book, his meaning of the word conversion probably became very evident . . . forgiveness, peace, love, reconciliation, prayer, penance . . . and he is totally aware of the results they have brought forth. Early on in the apparitions, as the throngs of conversions began to take place, he experienced these results in a profound way. He states:

"It seemed like a whole new world. People were joyfully singing and praying and celebrating. They were talking about the apparitions in factories and giving testimonies at meetings. And they were imprisoned for that. But they were coming out of prison glad that they could testify.

"It was not only me who went to prison, people were going before and after me. It didn't bother us at all! We were joyful—we felt that it should be that way."

Father Jozo simply lives a definition of conversion in its simplest and purest form. Make "Jesus" the most important part of your life . . . and renew it every day. It originated from Our Lady, who always leads to Jesus.

THE REIHLE FOUNDATION

BACKGROUND

(On the statue of Our Lady in Father Jozo's church.)

The present church at Tihaljina was constructed in the nineteen sixties. At that time, the parish priest had visited Rome where he discovered and fell in love with this remarkable image of Our Lady. Since his new church was then under construction, he felt this new found replica of Our Lady must become part of his parish. He ordered one shipped from Rome.

Under Communist rule, churches have no support from any governmental agency, and all construction costs must be privately funded. Such was the case at Tihaljina where parishioners struggled to raise enough contributions, which, coupled with providing their own labor, could complete their project. Efforts there are usually made all the more difficult because most of the parishioners are poor, living in an economy that is severely limited.

It must have been a great shock and disappointment then, when they discovered upon arrival of the statue, that the shipping costs, special tariffs, and import taxes being charged by the government were almost as much as the cost of the construction of the church building. Would it be that this beautiful image of Our Lady would be returned to Italy, or worse yet, left to slowly disintegrate on the docks of the port?

Special efforts, and obvious extreme sacrifices were made by the parishioners, who succeeded in collecting enough funds to release the statue and allow Our Lady to continue her journey to the new church. Now, twenty years later, people from all over the world are enriched by its presence.

THE
RIEHLE
FOUNDATION...

The Riehle Foundation is a non-profit, tax-exempt, charitable organization that exists to produce and/or distribute Catholic material to anyone, anywhere.

The Foundation is dedicated to the Mother of God and her role in the salvation of mankind. We believe that this role has not diminished in our time, but, on the contrary has become all the more apparent in this the era of Mary as recognized by Pope John Paul II, whom we strongly support.

During the past two years the foundation has distributed over one million books, films, rosaries, bibles, etc. to individuals, parishes, and organizations all over the world. Additionally, the foundation sends materials to missions and parishes in a dozen foreign countries.

Donations forwarded to The Riehle Foundation for the materials distributed provide our sole support. We appreciate your assistance, and request your prayers.

IN THE SERVICE OF JESUS AND MARY
All for the honor and glory of God!

The Riehle Foundation
P.O. Box 7
Milford, OH 45150

Thank You

We wish to thank Mr. Tony Cilento for permission to use the color photographs on the cover and inside pages of this book. A professional photographer, Tony has compiled thousands of slides on Medjugorje as part of a presentation titled "Portrait of Our Lady." For information about the pictures contact:

> TONY CILENTO STUDIOS
> 1409 E. Capitol Drive
> Milwaukee, WI 53211

We also wish to thank Michael Hall, Anne McGlone, Drew Marion, Helen Sarcevic, Sr. Charla Gannon, Dean and others for their encouragement and cooperation in providing their witnesses, black and white photographs and copies of Father Jozo's talks used in this book.

THE RIEHLE FOUNDATION